SUSTAINING PLACES:
THE ROLE OF THE COMPREHENSIVE PLAN

David R. Godschalk, FAICP, and William R. Anderson, FAICP

TABLE OF CONTENTS

CHAPTER 1

Introduction:
Task Force Charge and Approach

 This PAS Report arises from the Sustaining Places Initiative and the Sustaining Places Task Force created by APA in 2010 to define the role of comprehensive planning in addressing the sustainability of human settlement.

As stated by APA president Bruce Knight, FAICP, "Sustaining Places will examine both how places can be sustained and how places themselves sustain life and civilizations. Planning's comprehensive focus is not limited to a building or a site but encompasses all scales and all forms of organization of human settlement, from rural areas and small towns to cities and metropolitan regions. The challenges of sustainability and possible solutions require planners' values, skills, and leadership."

Regions, cities, and towns are where most people live and work, where most resources are consumed, and where most impacts to the environment, the economy, and society are generated. The Sustaining Places Task Force was charged with exploring the role of the comprehensive plan as the leading policy document and tool to help communities of all sizes achieve sustainable outcomes. A secondary charge was to examine related changes in the practice of planning, including best practices that integrate sustainability into the comprehensive planning process. Finally, the task force examined how comprehensive plans effect change and are evaluated and held accountable.

This report is directed to a broad audience, including not only planners but also citizens and decision makers interested in learning about and implementing comprehensive plans that sustain places.

SUSTAINING PLACES: CHALLENGES AND OPPORTUNITIES

Sustainability challenges are heightened by the need to act now to reduce the danger of climate change, as documented in the 2009 federal government report *Global Climate Change Impacts in the United States*. This report concluded that global warming is unequivocal and human-induced, and that climate-related impacts will include stress on water resources and agriculture, sea-level rise, drought, and risks to human health.

Global warming in and of itself is not the issue; rather, the issues are the manifold and complex climate changes global warming is inducing and the extraordinary rate of change already apparent. If this rate of change does not slow, the long-term implications for our communities and the planet could be severe—not just ecologically but also economically and socially. Even if one is skeptical of the science behind human-induced climate change, many other arguments exist for acting to achieve sustainability:

• Our communities and economies are almost completely dependent on a global market of increasingly expensive fossil fuels, with no cheap energy substitutes available in the quantities and applications needed for the foreseeable future.

• Many natural resources we rely on are already stressed by overuse (e.g., many ocean fisheries) and, in some cases, also by shifting climate patterns (e.g., water resources in the U.S. southwest).

• Continued global population growth and the explosive economic growth of China, India, Brazil, and other emerging economies further complicate the task of addressing our world's resource needs.

Planning for sustainability is ultimately about managing the environmental and economic risks of the 21st century in a way that capitalizes on the opportunities for improving economic prosperity. This demands a fresh approach to plan making and implementation that focuses on balancing environmental, economic, and equity values. The comprehensive plan of the near past is not only outdated but could be counterproductive due to its narrow focus, silo-like topical structure, and failure to account for the full range of climate change and energy impacts. A well-executed comprehensive planning effort that includes sustainability goals and predisaster hazard mitigation actions should not only improve the quality of life in a community but also drastically reduce long-term fiscal maintenance and operational costs from repeated disaster-recovery episodes. For example, a national study of hazard mitigation found that mitigation returned four dollars in benefits from avoided losses for every dollar invested in mitigation (Godschalk et al. 2009).

PROCESS

To prepare this report, the task force organized itself around major topics, including forces affecting sustainability in cities and regions, traditional and alternative models of the comprehensive plan, planning scales from the community to the region, plan preparation and implementation processes, and best practices in comprehensive planning for sustaining places. In wrestling with the multiple popular uses of the term "sustainability," we opted for "planning for sustaining places" as our designation of the planning process and for "sustainable community" as designating the goal of that planning process.

As part of its work, the task force reviewed a broad selection of materials related to sustainability and plans for sustainable communities, cities, and regions. (See Appendix A for plans reviewed.) To evaluate best practices in planning for sustaining places, the task force looked at the history, evolution, and current status of integrating sustainability into comprehensive plans, identified important characteristics, and set forth some basic principles. It also considered what distinguishes a plan for sustaining places from a well-done, traditional comprehensive plan. Finally, while the task force acknowledged that the comprehensive plan is only one tool among many that communities can employ in seeking to become sustainable, it also argued that the comprehensive plan is one of the more important and valuable tools in the community arsenal.

PLANNING FOR SUSTAINING PLACES: A WORKING DEFINITION

The Brundtland Commission of the United Nations, in its final report in 1987, stated that "sustainable development" should meet the needs of the present without compromising the ability of future generations to meet their own needs. Since then, the definition of "sustainability" has expanded to include balance and coordination among the "Three Es" of environment, economy, and equity (sometimes stated as the "Three Ps" or "Triple Bottom Line" of planet, prosperity, and people), as well as development that minimizes its negative impact on the environment and other systems.

The Brundtland Commission focused on goals for the development process—meaning ongoing actions communities take as they grow and change over time. Our focus, which is on plans for sustaining the places inhabited by human communities—their physical, social, economic, and environmental habitats—is similar. While it is difficult to separate the goals and process from the plans and places, our focus leads us to emphasize the critical role of the comprehensive plan as the policy instrument for guiding planning for sustainable communities. This is because the plan—by design, tradition, and law—is "comprehensive," and communities can achieve sustainable outcomes only when they address them comprehensively and holistically.

After reviewing the sustainability literature and debates (including Berke and Conroy 2000; Godschalk 2004; Herman 2010; Jacobson and Hinds 2008; and Schilling 2010) and analyzing contemporary plans for sustainable communities, we propose the following definition of planning for sustaining places:

> Planning for "sustaining places" is a dynamic, democratic process through which communities plan to meet the needs of current and future generations without compromising the ecosystems upon which they depend by balancing social, economic, and environmental resources, incorporating resilience and linking local actions to regional and global concerns.

Based on this definition, it is possible to identify the characteristics that distinguish plans for sustainable communities and to formulate principles to guide the practice of planning for sustaining places.

CHARACTERISTICS OF PLANS FOR SUSTAINABLE COMMUNITIES

As the definition indicates, one would expect to find in most plans for sustainable communities the following guides to action:

- *Plan dynamically and democratically.* Planning for sustaining places is an ongoing process based on continuous evaluation and monitoring, vigorous citizen participation and conflict resolution, and regular plan updating to ensure that citizens and decision makers are kept abreast of evolving scientific knowledge and community development issues.

- *Meet the needs of future generations.* Plans for sustaining places take special care to ensure that the needs of future generations are woven into their goals and not overlooked in the process of dealing with the needs of current generations, based on consideration of long-range projections and development scenarios.

- *Coordinate social, economic, and environmental systems.* Planning for sustaining places shapes private and public projects to balance potentially competing social, economic, and environmental objectives, even if this means placing higher priorities on social and environmental outcomes sometimes undervalued by the market.

- *Incorporate resilience.* Planning for sustaining places fosters resilient communities, economies, built environments, and natural ecosystems so they are able to anticipate, adapt to, and recover from disastrous impacts from extreme weather events, energy shortages, natural and man-made disasters, and other destabilizing events, as well as longer-term shifts in climate patterns, energy resources, and economic activity.

- *Link local, regional, and global concerns.* Planning for sustaining places acknowledges and accounts for reciprocal influences between local actions and the larger issues of regional, national, and global environments, economies, and equity.

While some of these basic characteristics are also found in many traditional comprehensive plans prepared prior to the emergence of sustainability concerns, traditional plans often have not dealt successfully with economic, environmental, community, and disaster resilience, and they have not looked beyond the local level to incorporate regional and global environment, economy, and equity issues.

Traditional plans have focused even less on the following defining characteristics of planning for sustaining places, which are found in leading contemporary plans for sustaining places:

- Adopting sustainability principles to guide planning and decision making and to drive innovation to close existing gaps in sustainability—formally committing the community to sustainability as a high priority.

- Coordinating and integrating policies and actions from separate functional plans (such as climate change, hazard mitigation, community health, housing, environmental quality, food security, and others) into the overall framework of the comprehensive plan—bringing together the content of these often stand-alone plans made in response to federal or state mandates or to the missions of nongovernmental or professional organizations.

- Influencing development decisions so as to improve and to sustain people's livelihoods, their living and working places, and their environmental resources by ensuring fair distribution of benefits and burdens and equitable access to public facilities—moving beyond the physical environment to consider the impact of development proposals on community wellbeing, health, equity, and quality of life.

- Acting on scientific evidence regarding anticipated changes in global economic and environmental systems and their local consequences through mitigation and adaptation—actively monitoring the findings of relevant scientific studies and basing community actions on them.

- Recognizing the need to address multiple sustainability demands with limited funds in times of fiscal stress—weighing difficult choices and consequences and prioritizing plan implementation to coordinate sustainability objectives with ongoing public programs.

- Implementing sustainability goals that extend beyond the scope, format, and techniques of the traditional comprehensive plan—planning to cope with an increasingly uncertain future, much of it unfolding on a continuous basis and determined globally rather than locally.

- Identifying and monitoring sustainability metrics in order to measure progress toward reaching plan goals and objectives and to inform decision makers and the community about the status of sustainability issues—ensuring that stakeholders are aware of how well their plans are meeting their needs.

- Making explicit linkages to regional plans and actions in order to incorporate environmental and economic processes operating beyond the local scale—coordinating with regional planning and development agencies to strengthen joint initiatives.

- Promoting collaborative multistakeholder processes that engage the full range of community interests and leaders so as to ensure public involvement and education about sustainability issues and needs—enabling informed decisions by policy makers and citizens about plan priorities and implementation.

What distinguishes the practice of planning for sustaining places? What foundational principles underlie plans for sustainable communities? Based on the above characteristics and on reviews of leading plans for sustainable communities, Chapter 2 proposes a set of principles to guide the preparation of plans for sustaining places.

Principles of Planning
for Sustaining Places

 Planning for sustainability is the defining challenge of the 21st century. Overcoming deeply ingrained economic and cultural patterns that result in resource depletion, climate instability, and economic and social stress requires holistic problem solving that blends the best scientific understanding of existing conditions and available technologies with the public resolve to act. Planning processes allow communities to look past immediate concerns, to evaluate options for how best to proceed, and to move toward a better future.

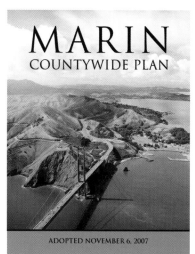

MARIN
COUNTYWIDE PLAN

ADOPTED NOVEMBER 6, 2007

Marin County

The comprehensive plan has the legal authority to act as the vehicle for guiding community development, the scope to cover the necessary functions and facilities, and the history of practice to inspire public acceptance of its policies. While the plan is not the only tool that communities are using to improve sustainability (Quay 2010), it has the advantage of being able to integrate long- and short-range perspectives and to coordinate other policies, plans, and programs into a single accessible document. Planning can provide the necessary analysis, the requisite communitywide education and reflection, and the momentum required to respond to these monumental challenges.

Sustainability issues of climate, natural resources, community health, energy production and consumption, lifecycle costs of public investments, and long-term viability of environmental systems, in combination with land use, transportation, community character, urban form, economic prosperity, and many other traditional comprehensive plan attributes, make the planning process challenging. Expertise is required to effectively decipher, understand, and explain the relationships between these issues and attributes. With the growing acknowledgment of the need to create sustainable communities, planners have an increasingly difficult and important role. Traditional plans are not well suited to respond to these broader challenges.

There is growing evidence, however, that North American planning is taking up this sustainability challenge.

- Comprehensive plans from a wide range of communities have been reformulated to focus on sustaining places. Plans from places as diverse as Marin County, California; Fort Collins, Colorado; Burlington, Vermont; Union County, Ohio; Philadelphia; Seattle; San Diego; Albany, New York; and Cleveland make sustainability an overriding goal (see Appendix A).

- New metrics to measure sustainability have been created and used to assess the effectiveness of plans for sustaining places (Feiden 2011).

- The planning literature is now replete with articles describing new approaches to sustaining places, including places in decline as well as those that are growing (Schilling and Logan 2008).

- The autumn 2010 special issue of the *Journal of the American Planning Association* dealt with planning for climate change.

- States such as California have enacted and implemented a new suite of laws (see California Sustainable Communities Strategy, California Senate Bill 375 [2008], and California Assembly Bill 32 [2006]) directing local governments to plan and carry out actions to enhance their sustainability.

- A proliferation of governmental associations and nonprofit organizations dedicated to working toward sustainability has arisen (e.g., the STAR program of ICLEI–Local Governments for Sustainability, a membership organization of local governments committed to advancing climate protection and sustainable development; see www.icleiusa.org/star).

- Within APA, the new Sustainable Community Planning Interest Group has enlisted more than 1,000 planners who are dedicated to orienting their practice toward sustaining places (see http://blogs.planning.org/sustainability/2011/02/17/apas-sustainable-community-planning-interest-group).

- In support of the planning communities' response, the Federal Partnership for Sustainable Communities has funded Regional Plans for Sustainable Development (see www.sustainablecommunities.gov).

Clearly, a sea change is taking place.

How did we arrive at this new juncture in planning history? Planning for sustaining places has its roots in growth management initiatives that sought to guide development into desirable urban patterns, rather than simply responding to individual development requests (Meck 2002). More recent approaches, such as Smart Growth (Smart Growth Network 2002) and new urbanism (www.cnu.org), aim to shift conventional planning practice from organizing physical community growth to making well-informed and equitable decisions about resource use, aesthetics, and quality of life. As evidence mounted that climate change, ecosystem stress, the end of cheap fossil fuels, and global economic shifts were affecting local jurisdictions in new and more negative ways, it was a natural next step for planners to broaden and to build on these concepts through conscious use of goal-oriented principles aimed at creating and maintaining more sustainable communities and regions.

IMPLICATIONS FOR PLANNING PRACTICE

What does this shift toward sustaining places mean for planning practice? This chapter develops the distinguishing principles of comprehensive planning for sustaining places. These principles are based on a review and synthesis of comprehensive plans completed over the past decade that substantially integrate sustainability in a variety of ways into the planning process and resulting plans. (See Appendix A for a more detailed discussion of those plans.) The resulting window on the best practices in planning for sustaining places can become the profession's starting point for developing and improving the practice.

Ours is not the first effort to define guiding principles for planning for sustainable communities. In 2000, APA adopted its Policy Guide on Planning for Sustainability, which set out a strategy with four objectives:

1. Reduce dependence upon fossil fuels and extracted underground metals and minerals.

2. Reduce dependence on chemicals and other manufactured substances that can accumulate in Nature.

3. Reduce dependence on activities that harm life-sustaining ecosystems.

4. Meet the hierarchy of present and future needs fairly and efficiently.

In PAS Report 565, *Assessing Sustainability*, Wayne Feiden summarized a range of other attempts to define sustainability in operative terms that apply to planning (Feiden 2011, 19–25). He describes principles put forth by this task force, as well as those published by a number of other organizations, including the President's Council on Sustainable Development's definitions (1997), APA's PAS Report no. 479, *The Principles of Smart Development* (1998), the Smart Growth Network's reports on smart growth (2002 and 2003), the American Institute of Architects' 10 Principles for Livable Communities, the ICLEI–Local Governments for Sustainability's Star Community Index (see sidebar, page 10), and the Massachusetts Office for Commonwealth Development's 10 Sustainable Development Principles.

Feiden approves of the 1997 definition by the President's Council on Sustainable Development: "Sustainable communities are cities and towns that prosper because people work together to produce a high quality of life that they want to sustain and constantly improve. They are communities that flourish because they build a mutually supportive, dynamic balance between social wellbeing, economic opportunity, and environmental quality" (http://clinton2.nara.gov/PCSD). He points out the similarity between sustainability principles and the principles of smart growth, as

STAR COMMUNITY INDEX—A NEW TOOL FOR DEFINING COMMUNITY-SCALE SUSTAINABILITY

In October 2010, ICLEI released its STAR Index Sustainability Goals and Guiding Principles as its first step in establishing a strategic planning and performance management system intended to serve as a road map for communities incorporating sustainability into their planning framework. It includes 81 goals and 10 guiding principles used to define and evaluate community-scale sustainability across eight specific categories.

The categories, contained within the three overarching topics of environment, economy, and society, are:

1. *Environment*
   - Natural systems
   - Planning and design
   - Energy and climate

2. *Economy*
   - Economic prosperity
   - Employment and workforce training

3. *Society*
   - Education, arts, and community
   - Health and safety
   - Affordability and social equity

STAR is intended as a rating system, a tool for communities to evaluate their own progress against a series of performance and best-practice measures. Its structure is based on a set of components that will allow for incorporation of a variety of measures—both qualitative as well as quantitative. The framework includes the following elements:

- Goal—a descriptive title for a desired outcome a jurisdiction intends to achieve, such as "green infrastructure" or "compact and complete community"

- Purpose—a statement to clarify relevance, to provide context, and to communicate the desired outcome

- Validation measure—either a performance measure (defined as a verifiable indicator or metric, either qualitative or quantitative, to be used to identify progress relative to the goal) or a practice measure (defined as an action, practice, or systematic approach to be used to move toward the goal)

Validation measures are being developed by a series of committees during 2011. In 2012, ICLEI will release a pilot version of the STAR Community Index system as an online set of tools that will allow STAR to be used as a more complete sustainability planning and performance measuring system. In the meantime, many communities have begun using the goals and guiding principles as an organizing framework for their sustainability planning efforts, so that they will be in alignment with STAR as the program is further developed.

Source: www.icleiusa.org/star

stated in the Livability Principles of the Federal Partnership for Sustainable Communities, which include providing more transportation choices, promoting equitable and affordable housing, enhancing economic competitiveness, supporting existing communities, coordinating and leveraging federal policies and investment, and valuing communities and neighborhoods.

The principles identified in Feiden's review are familiar to those in urban and regional planning and community governance. They build on accepted principles of growth management and good planning. But we believe that, when focused on community sustainability as an overriding goal and when seriously implemented, they take planning practice to a new, higher level of commitment, comprehensiveness, and coverage. To inform this new generation of comprehensive plans for sustaining places, our aim is to translate the sustainable communities and livability principles into best-practice guidance specifically tailored for comprehensive-plan making. For our purposes, best practices are distilled from among the best current plans; this choice does not imply that these are "ideal" practices, that they are without controversy, or that these places have achieved sustainability. Rather, they represent the best available efforts to date.

BEST-PRACTICE PRINCIPLES FOR SUSTAINING PLACES COMPREHENSIVE PLANS

From our review of the literature and our knowledge of planning practice, we identified eight principles for best practices that can guide the making of comprehensive plans for sustaining places (expanded from Berke and Conroy 2000). These principles are categorized thus:

1. Livable Built Environment

2. Harmony with Nature

3. Resilient Economy

4. Interwoven Equity

5. Healthy Community

6. Responsible Regionalism

7. Authentic Participation

8. Accountable Implementation

To test the principles and to evaluate their application as best practices in planning for sustainable places, it is important to evaluate the degree to which they actually inform the making of plans. We assessed the state of practice for sustaining places by analyzing representative comprehensive plans and planning processes that contain examples of best practice at various scales—city, county, region—in different geographical locations and relative to different types of population change (growing, stable, and contracting). In preparing this report, we analyzed the following plans and processes (reviewed in Appendix A):

- Toward a Sustainable Seattle (2005)

- Marin Countywide Plan (2007)

- Plan Fort Collins (2011)

- Regional Comprehensive Plan for the San Diego Region (2004)

- Keene, New Hampshire, Comprehensive Master Plan (2010)

- Burlington, Vermont, Legacy Plan (2000)

- Union County, Pennsylvania, Cultivating Community Comprehensive Plan (2009)

- Philadelphia 2035 Plan

- Connecting Cleveland 2020 Citywide Plan (2007)

- Albany 2030 Comprehensive Plan

Each principle is defined and discussed below, along with instances illustrating how the principle is employed in the goals and policies of the plans, as well as lists of specific actions or criteria that follow from the principle.

Livable Built Environment

The livable built environment principle states that the goals and policies of a plan for sustaining places should ensure that all elements of the built environment, including land use, transportation, housing, energy, and infrastructure, work together to provide sustainable, green places for living, working, and recreation, with a high quality of life.

Urban development has the capacity to harm or enhance community livability, depending on the design and goals of individual projects as well as public policies and infrastructure investments. Plans for sustainable places set frameworks for transportation, land use, and housing that not only integrate goals for walkable neighborhoods, accessible and multimodal travel systems, and a range of housing types but also address new topics, such as community health and wellness, energy conservation and efficiency, food supply, climate change mitigation and adaptation, and others. The influence of this principle was evident in all of the plans reviewed. For example, the Seattle comprehensive plan seeks a livable built environment through its Urban Villages Strategy, which establishes a typology of dense activity centers based on accommodating future population and job growth targets within mixed use, walkable neighborhoods. The plan emphasizes an integrated approach of land use and transportation, combining principles of smart growth, urban design, and public participation. The Fort Collins comprehensive plan addresses the built environment in a section on community and neighborhood livability, as well as in its transportation section.

Best practices for meeting the livable built environments principle are to:

- Provide transportation choices, including pedestrian and bike path systems

- Encourage and enable transit-oriented development

- Design complete streets that serve multiple functions and modes

- Coordinate regional transportation with job clusters

- Promote mixed land use at different scales

- Make efficient use of existing infrastructure by encouraging infill development

- Ensure a range of housing types

- Provide fair access to quality public facilities and spaces

- Design walkable neighborhoods

- Conserve and reuse historic resources

- Carry out neighborhood revitalization

- Implement low-impact development

- Set green building standards

- Use renewable energy systems

- Establish urban design standards

- Avoid development in areas prone to natural hazards

Harmony with Nature

The harmony with nature principle states that the goals and policies of a plan for sustaining places should ensure that the contributions of natural resources to human well-being are explicitly recognized and valued and that maintaining their health is a primary objective.

Ecological systems typically suffer the most from urban development; as open space and habitats are reduced and human activity and wastes are introduced, air and water quality decline, and both ecological resources and local and migratory species are affected. Plans for sustaining places employ environmental inventories and analyses to adopt sustainability standards, incorporate best-practice approaches to the management of systems needed to support communities, and prepare land-use plans and regulations to maintain the health of natural systems as a primary priority. All of the plans reviewed for this report paid careful attention to the principle of harmony with nature. For example, the Natural Systems and Agriculture element

© iStockphoto.com/Richard Gunion

Natural and man-made systems come together in Harpers Ferry, West Virginia, and communities nationwide.

of the Marin Countywide Plan addresses biological and water resources, environmental hazards, atmosphere and climate, and open space. It sets goals to minimize the use of finite resources, to use all resources efficiently and effectively, to reduce use of hazardous materials, to reduce greenhouse gas (GHG) emissions, to preserve natural assets, and to protect agricultural assets. The Keene, New Hampshire, Comprehensive Master Plan includes a vision focus area, A Unique Natural Environment, which addresses natural areas as well as man-made green infrastructure. It is particularly strong in addressing climate change, with a process to reduce GHG emissions by 10 percent by 2015. The Albany 2030 Comprehensive Plan addresses waterways, stormwater management, brownfield sites, urban forest, and air quality; its utilities section covers energy and green building. The San Diego Association of Government's 2004 Regional Comprehensive Plan and the 2008 City of San Diego General Plan each reinforce their region's Multiple Species Conservation Plans for large and connected open space areas preserved to sustain critical habitat for endangered and threatened species.

Best practices for meeting the harmony with nature principle are to:

- Protect critical habitat or sensitive lands from development

- Reduce carbon footprints

- Restore and connect natural habitats and open lands

- Respect natural topography

- Meet air quality standards

- Achieve climate protection goals

- Increase energy security

- Commit to green building

- Reduce solid waste volumes

- Restore streams and manage watersheds and floodplains

- Manage stormwater quality and quantity

- Conserve resources, including energy, water, and natural open space

- Implement responsible stewardship for open lands, natural areas, and wildlife habitat

- Integrate renewable energy into energy sources

- Maintain a lasting water supply

Resilient Economy

The resilient economy principle states that the goals and policies of a plan for sustaining places should ensure that the community is prepared to deal with both positive and negative changes in its economic health and to initiate sustainable urban development and redevelopment strategies that foster business growth and build reliance on local assets.

Local and regional economic ups and downs, as well as long-term national and international economic changes, affect the prospects for community development. Plans for sustainable places document the underlying economic conditions and provide a vehicle for community response to either growth or decline, including initiating programs to develop green and clean-tech businesses and jobs. They also work to align economic plans and strategies with other community goals and to build public-private partnerships aimed at developing economies that can weather the impacts of changing situations, such as the economic downturns and foreclosures occurring in many neighborhoods (Hollander 2011). This is a relatively new principle, but it is increasingly appearing in comprehensive plans. For example, a foundational principle of the Burlington, Vermont, Legacy Plan is to maintain the city as a regional population, government, cultural, and economic center with livable wage jobs, full employment, social supports, and housing that matches job growth and family income. The City of San Diego Plan's Economic Prosperity Element has a Prime Industrial Land policy to protect capacity for its manufacturing, technology, logistics, and research and development industries to respond and thrive. On the other hand, the Philadelphia comprehensive plan responds to its history as a shrinking city in its THRIVE section, which identifies former industrial areas for redevelopment, combined with colocation of public services and amenities and expanded housing options. And sustainability stands out as the dominant motif of the 2007 Connecting Cleveland 2020 Citywide Plan, as it outlines wealth creation and adaptive reuse strategies to reverse the impacts of population and economic decline.

Best practices for meeting the resilient economy principle are to:

- Provide physical capacity for economic growth

- Maintain a balanced land-use mix to support fiscal sustainability

- Plan for commercial and industrial land development and job creation

- Identify and promote commercial and industrial lands in need of redevelopment

- Plan convenient and affordable transportation and transit systems for access to employment centers

- Identify, develop, and support a region's comparative advantages

- Encourage green businesses and support green jobs

- Promote local ownership and production of goods and services, when appropriate

- Respond to regional retail and employment competition

- Implement community-based economic development
- Develop action plans for neighborhoods at risk
- Provide diverse jobs with competitive wages
- Create or foster an innovative and entrepreneurial atmosphere
- Build partnerships with educational institutions
- Ensure fiscal sustainability and transparency
- Design and build infrastructure efficiently to stay cost competitive
- Make advance plans for postdisaster economic recovery

Interwoven Equity

The interwoven equity principle states that the goals and policies of a plan for sustaining places should ensure fairness and equity in providing for the housing, services, health, safety, and livelihood needs of all citizens and groups.

This principle holds that attention to the fair distribution of costs and benefits should be present in every part of a plan for sustaining places. Individual development proposals are designed to further the interests of their proposers, often regardless of the impact on other community stakeholders. Plans for sustainable places advocate for the needs of other affected groups, especially those who lack the power or resources to ensure that their needs are met, by imposing criteria for fairness and equity in the development process. Land-use, transportation, and urban form decisions should facilitate equitable access and distribution of resources.

This principle is increasingly important as socioeconomic gaps between the "haves" and "have nots" widen. For example, the goals of the Marin Countywide Plan are to supply housing affordable to all members of the workforce and diverse community, to educate and prepare the workforce and residents, to cultivate ethnic, cultural, and socioeconomic diversity, and to support public health, safety, and social justice. Through its Communities of Choice principle, the Connecting Cleveland 2020 Citywide Plan recognizes the need to create communities for those with few choices, as well as for those with many choices. And the Union County, Pennsylvania, Cultivating Community Comprehensive Plan addresses equity in several sections, including the provision of affordable housing and access to health care and community services.

Best practices for meeting the interwoven equity principle are to:

- Provide affordable and workforce housing
- Improve the physical, environmental, and economic health of disadvantaged neighborhoods
- Ensure jobs-housing coordination
- Improve health of at-risk populations
- Include underserved populations in the planning process
- Provide accessible and quality public services to minority and low-income neighborhoods
- Improve and add infrastructure and facilities to areas with older or substandard public facilities
- Protect vulnerable neighborhoods from natural hazards
- Promote diversity in the workplace

- Measure plan objectives and outcomes to determine the equitable distribution of benefits and costs

Healthy Community

The healthy community principle states that the goals and policies of a plan for sustaining places should ensure that public health needs are recognized and addressed through provisions for healthy foods, physical activity, access to recreation, health care, environmental justice, and safe neighborhoods.

The healthy community principle addresses the public health implications of land-use, transportation, housing, food production, and other plan proposals. Research has shown that certain kinds of urban form can have negative impacts on human health by encouraging sedentary lifestyles and failing to provide access to healthy foods. Planning for sustainable places promotes public health, healthy eating, and physical activity through plans that support walking and other outdoor activities, accessible recreation and health care, protection of agricultural land, and encouragement of local food production. This is a newer principle for comprehensive planning; it would not have appeared in most 20th-century plans, but it is increasingly evident in plans for sustainable communities. For example, the Fort Collins, Colorado, comprehensive plan includes an element that addresses community health and safety, as well as local food access and production. The Healthy Community section of the Keene, New Hampshire, plan focuses on how a healthy and safe community can provide for both individual and community health and well-being, access to health care, and resources to lead safe, healthy lives.

Best practices for meeting the healthy communities principle are to:

- Ensure that all people live in a safe and healthy environment

- Reduce barriers to opportunities for physical activity and active lifestyles

- Provide an adequate amount of recreational space and opportunities for all residents

- Locate parks, greenways, and open space accessible to neighborhoods

- Encourage access to locally grown healthy food

- Improve health and wellness, especially of at-risk populations

- Ensure that adequate schools are provided for all neighborhoods

- Mitigate brownfield sites

- Provide access to affordable health care facilities

- Support the arts and cultural facilities

- Design for walking and biking to destinations

- Implement environmental justice programs to protect poor neighborhoods from environmental pollution

Responsible Regionalism

The responsible regionalism principle states that the goals and policies of a plan for sustaining places should ensure that all local proposals account for, connect with, and support the plans of adjacent jurisdictions and the surrounding region.

Despite the regional nature of many urban systems—such as transportation, housing and labor markets, and watersheds—many community plans stop at the city limits, failing to work collaboratively with those of neighboring places. Plans for sustainable places work within the context of regional resources and facilities to coordinate goals and programs across jurisdictional boundaries. This principle is one of the more difficult to follow, given the weak nature of regional planning institutions in the United States; a limited number of the plans reviewed had been able to achieve effective regional coordination. The San Diego County Regional Comprehensive Plan is an exception; it effectively integrates regional comprehensive, transportation, and open space plans, and coordinates them with local plans through participatory planning, goal setting, funding programs, and sustainability measures. The Union County, Pennsylvania, plan emphasizes intracounty regional approaches through multimunicipal planning and regionalization of services, but contains limited policies for coordination with surrounding jurisdictions.

Best practices for meeting the responsible regionalism principle are to:

- Coordinate local land-use, open space, and mobility plans with regional plans in a connected and integrated regional network

- Enhance connections between city activity centers and regional destinations

- Participate in regional "greenprint" plans

- Participate in regional fair-share housing allocations

- Link local population and economic projections with regional projections

- Coordinate regional infrastructure priorities and funding

- Partner with leaders from adjacent jurisdictions to define regional needs and priorities

- Involve local jurisdictions in preparation of regional development visions and plans

- Share fiscal resources and responsibilities to implement plans

- Involve private-sector, nonprofit, and interest groups in regional planning efforts

- Coordinate with state and federal agencies during plan development

- Coordinate conservation efforts and plans for natural resource and critical habitat preservation

Authentic Participation

The authentic participation principle states that the goals and policies of a plan for sustaining places should ensure that the planning process actively involves all segments of the community in analyzing issues, generating visions, developing plans, and monitoring outcomes.

Democratic participation in planning and decision making faces a number of obstacles and challenges due to the increasingly complex and uncertain nature of the relevant scientific evidence on anticipated impacts, as well as inherent fear of change and concern for protecting neighborhoods. Because plans for sustaining places often demand major changes in community goals and behavior, it is important to bring representatives of all affected stakeholder groups (including those who do not typically participate) to the planning table throughout the process, from vision setting to implementation and monitoring for accountability.

This principle is widely recognized and creatively applied in the plans reviewed. For example, the Burlington, Vermont, Legacy Plan used outreach to community groups, neighborhoods, and a youth delegation to develop its plan, and the plan's progress is reviewed against its goals annually at a town meeting. To build support for its Urban Villages Strategy, Seattle empowered neighborhood planning groups to devise village plans and gave them funding and technical assistance to implement the Sustainable Seattle Strategy.

Best practices to meet the authentic participation principle are to:

- Carry out citywide and neighborhood participatory planning programs

- Seek broad and diverse participation, including people from all generations

- Build organized constituencies for plan making and outcome monitoring

- Use participation techniques geared to different population groups

- Involve representatives of all stakeholder groups

- Provide ongoing information on planning issues, events, and outcomes

- Use social media to educate and to involve a wide range of interests

- Promote leadership development in disadvantaged communities

- Ensure that staff of responsible agencies are involved with the public

- Design an open and transparent planning decision-making process

- Formulate alternative vision scenarios and evaluate their outcomes to inform public decision making

Accountable Implementation

The accountable implementation principle states that the goals and policies of a plan for sustaining places should ensure that responsibilities for carrying out the plan are clearly stated, along with metrics for evaluating progress in achieving desired outcomes.

Because of their broad scope and multiple effects and the lead time necessary to fund, design, and execute them, comprehensive planning proposals often take a long time to realize, making measurable implementation difficult. Plans for sustainable places build in benchmarks, indicators, targets, and other metrics that track progress and adjust strategies on an ongoing basis. They assign specific responsibilities for, monitor performance on, and provide effective tools for meeting targets to ensure that the public and elected officials understand both achievements and shortfalls. This implementation principle would not have been apparent in most 20th-century comprehensive plans; the rise of metrics for measuring and reporting plan successes and failures is strikingly obvious in the plans reviewed for this report.

For example, the Albany 2030 Plan uses a systems approach to identify priorities for implementation that draws on community inputs, connections among plan systems, and effective intervention points. The Philadelphia 2035 Plan envisions the development of 18 district plans to be prepared at the neighborhood scale and includes a detailed cost matrix with estimates of capital and operating costs of all plan strategies, lists of responsible agencies, and an implementation timeframe. Implementation of the San Diego Regional Comprehensive Plan is facilitated by proceeds from a half-cent sales tax that helps fund implementation of the corresponding Regional Transportation Plan and the Environmental Mitigation Program in accordance with the Smart Growth Concept Map used to prioritize transportation investments and funding for infrastructure improvements; it includes a five-year action plan and a performance monitoring program.

Best practices to meet the accountable implementation principle are to:

- Involve the public in setting goals and objectives

- Coordinate all organizations and agencies with implementation responsibilities

- Develop indicators and metrics to measure goal achievement

- Balance needs to upgrade existing infrastructure with funding demands for new social services and green technology

- Assign responsibilities and set schedules for plan implementation

- Set priorities for plan-related public investments

- Commit the necessary public and private resources over time

- Involve community partners to achieve diverse implementation

- Monitor outcomes and progress toward planning goals

- Regularly report plan implementation progress to the public and decision makers, including during the annual budgeting process.

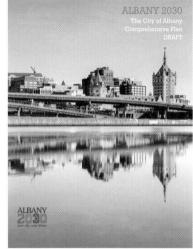

City of Albany

NEXT STEPS

Why do we need to make plans for sustainable communities? What underlies the need to focus on sustaining places in comprehensive plans? How can we make the case for reforming comprehensive planning to account for the challenges of climate change, energy shortages, and economic turbulence? Chapter 3 addresses the factors that call for a stronger and more focused sustainable places planning approach.

The Need for Sustainability
in Cities and Regions

 Sustainability is threatened by resource depletion, climate instability, and economic and social turbulence, which strain the balance among environmental, economic, and equity values. Dealing with these challenges imposes new demands on community planners, who are on the front lines in responding to the local impacts of these strains. Older, traditional comprehensive plans were hindered in coming to terms with these new demands due to the historic evolution of the plan into a technical tool to allocate future land use and infrastructure to accommodate projected community growth and to provide a framework for zoning and development regulations. Newer plans for sustaining places have the opportunity to broaden and to reformulate their missions in order to lead their communities toward sustainable futures.

The challenge of creating sustainable communities is equal parts technical and adaptive. Whereas technical challenges can be solved with expertise, technology, and best practices, adaptive challenges require group learning and decision making. While the temptation is to treat every challenge as a technical one with simple solutions that can be accumulated, the reality is that marked improvements in the creation of sustainable communities requires adaptive problem solving where both technical and nontechnical fixes are amplified by group learning about problems with unknown solutions. Here, the role of the planner shifts from technical expert to facilitator of public discussion. The comprehensive planning process is uniquely suited to facilitate the extremely complex discovery process necessary to shift the trajectories of our cities.

Downtown Cleveland

Sustainability influences the way plans are written in two important ways. The first influence results in a shift in mindset when the public process is underpinned by a dedication to sustainability. Citizens come to sustainability from many different perceptions and at different levels of interest and knowledge. Planners understand the connections among land use, transportation, environmental quality, economic development, neighborhoods, and the like, but the public attention may be focused on only one or two of these elements. Discussing with them the connections between urban systems can provide a more robust understanding of the implications of particular strategies or policy decisions. To this end, the new social media tools can be effective in reaching out to previously unengaged segments of the population, as evidenced in the Connecting Cleveland 2020 Citywide Plan. Thinking of implications for both present and future generations, along with a holistic definition of what sustainability means for a particular community, creates a good working mind-set for the planning process.

The second influence directly affects the plan document. Thoughtfully considering sustainability issues forces a truly integrated approach to problem solving that goes beyond just adding additional chapters to a plan. Furthermore, monitoring progress in one urban or environmental system while tracking its impacts on others calls for a plan that is much more dynamic. The challenge is not new to planners, but the force behind a sustainable approach magnifies the need for understanding the links between man-made and natural systems. The implication is that we need a serious reevaluation of the structure of the traditional comprehensive plan, moving beyond the standard elements (land use, transportation, housing, etc.) to topics that reflect the larger systems influencing sustainability, such as natural systems and agriculture, the built environment, and socioeconomic systems, as in the Marin Countywide Plan.

Few people read comprehensive plans from cover to cover; at the same time, citizens have easy access to more information than ever about both their own community and communities around the world through an ever-growing network of online tools. However, the information citizens want is not necessarily organized in a linear way. Carefully considering how a plan can be translated into nonlinear online forms for searching and referencing, as well as how to maximize the public's exposure to the content of the plan, can extend its usefulness and make it relevant in day-to-day decision making. Many municipalities provide access to digital versions of their plans, but the real innovators are completely altering the plan format to better suit the way the public is consuming information. It seems clear that plans of the future will continue that trend and begin to incorporate modeling and even gaming technologies to communicate the contents of future plans. The added functionality and flexibility of digital plan creation (rather than simple plan writing) greatly improves the relevance and longevity of plan recommendations. For example, see the California Planning Roundtable's Reinventing the General Plan project (http://reinventingthegeneralplan.org).

In many states, comprehensive plans are more than just visionary communication tools; they are part of the legal structure for land use. The Burnham Plan for Chicago or *Temporary Paradise* by Kevin Lynch and Donald Appleyard for San Diego, both privately sponsored endeavors, had the freedom to inspire and assert from the writers' and sponsors' perspectives, but they did not have the power of law, direct or indirect, that most comprehensive plans prepared by government agencies have today. Comprehensive plans today must inspire as well as provide the policy basis for regulations, discretionary decisions, and capital investments.

SUSTAINABILITY CONNECTIONS IN COMPREHENSIVE PLANNING

By their nature, comprehensive plans must stretch their attention across the many components of a sustainable community. The most familiar components deal with the physical environment: land use, transportation, and natural environment. Equally important are the contributions of green infrastructure, food and water, energy, resilience, and community and economic health.

Land Use, Transportation, Environment

Plans have tremendous potential to shape the quality of our living environments and the sustainability of our communities. Sprawling, car-dependent patterns of land development and urban form not only result in loss of land and natural habitats but also serve to increase energy consumption and our carbon footprint. Local and regional comprehensive plans that promote compact, mixed use, walkable environments—creating opportunities to walk and bicycle and spend more time outside and out of cars—have the reverse effects. The environmental, economic, and energy-use benefits of compact, contiguous development patterns are well established (EPA 2001).

Sustainable mobility planning seeks to create meaningful and practical alternatives to driving a car. Automobile dependence undermines long-term sustainability through negative effects on air quality, GHG emissions, excessive commitments of urban space, and local economic overdependence on fossil fuels. While automobile and fuel technology are improving through development of hybrids, electric vehicles, plug-in hybrids, and nonfossil fuels, automobile dependence still incurs high economic, social, and envi-

ronmental costs to both to individuals and the larger society. The per capita energy consumption (BTU per passenger mile) associated with private cars is dramatically higher than for public transit. Sustainable cities invest in a diverse and robust network of mobility options, from heavy rail, commuter rail, buses (including bus rapid transit), light rail, and streetcars to bicycling and walking. Sustainable small towns and rural areas, often lacking the densities to support internal public transit systems, may require different types of transportation investments that include transit linkages to employment and business centers in larger cities, as well as rely more on improved vehicle and fuel technologies. The physical form of a community can influence the feasibility of these sustainable forms of mobility. For example, comprehensive plans can create the framework for promoting transit-oriented development (TOD), where density and development are coordinated with and proximate to good transit, and can create the conditions for living a car-free or car-reduced life. Investing in more sustainable mobility infrastructure and urban form will also help cities and communities become more resilient in the face of the long-term depletion of cheap oil.

Planning for density and mixing of uses is important, but so is the design of complete streets (which provide space for bicycles and transit as well as for cars), shared spaces, and pedestrian networks and infrastructure. Community plans can create the context for stimulating and interesting pedestrian environments through streetscape investments and public art elements that encourage walking and time spent in the public realm.

Compact development patterns, with alternative and competitive choices for moving about, have fiscal benefits too. Less asphalt laid, fewer potholes to repair, and the saved opportunity cost of usurping potentially taxable land for nontaxable roadways and freeways are cost savings to taxpayers and developers who pay impact fees. Of course, these savings have to be weighed against the cost of developing and operating alternative forms of mobility, especially public transportation. Still, compact mixed use development patterns, in which people can choose to live close to where they work and commute by biking or walking, clearly require less infrastructure expenditure per capita. Compact and integrated urban forms support not only alternatives to the automobile and its GHG emissions but also the future evolution of automobile and fuel technologies that rely less on fossil fuels, such as electric vehicles and plug-in hybrids that have more limited ranges between charges until battery storage technology catches up.

The design of buildings and infrastructure also represents a significant opportunity to reduce environmental and energy impacts. Green building standards (e.g., minimum LEED certification or comparable state building codes such as California's recently implemented Green Building Standards Code) are increasingly common, for instance, and green-building goals and targets are often included in comprehensive plans (e.g., Seattle's comprehensive plan sets a target for all new public buildings to be carbon neutral by 2030). Even bolder design concepts show the potential for change, as there are now many new examples of structures that use extremely little energy (e.g., "Passivhaus," which is quickly becoming a standard in Europe) or produce as much as or more energy than they require ("zero net energy" or "positive energy"). Urban sustainability and historic preservation are increasingly viewed as complementary; when we protect an older structure, we are conserving the embodied energy in the building materials of that structure, as well as its history, charm, and character.

One vision of a complete street

Charlotte Department of Transportation

Goods, Water, and Food

Modern cities require large resource flows to sustain their lifestyles and economic production. These material flows—analogous to the metabolism of a living organism—include a variety of essential community "inputs" (among them energy, food, water, and building materials) and generate a host of "outputs" in the form of municipal solid waste, air and water pollution, and GHG emissions. These material flows have become increasingly unsustainable for a variety of reasons (Sheehan and Spiegelman 2010). Both raw materials and finished goods regularly come from hundreds or thousands of miles away, with little recognition of their environmental impacts along the way; the "ecological footprint" concept provides one measure of these impacts (Wackernagel and Rees 1998). Urban sustainability demands a rethinking of this metabolism, shifting from a linear flow to a circular flow in which waste is creatively reused, where more inputs such as food and energy are produced locally, and where the size of these flows is reduced (e.g., reducing the energy consumption of buildings). Comprehensive plans with a sustainability focus will have many opportunities to advance a more sustainable resource metabolism.

Water is another special area of concern. Cities' growth patterns and policies dramatically influence the use and waste of water, particularly the conservation and protection of sources of drinking water (e.g., aquifers and river systems). Much water can be conserved, for instance, by reducing the extent of conventional suburban lawns and by shifting to xeriscaping and low-water, drought-resistant native vegetation. Compact development patterns result in less water consumption per household (see, e.g., Kenway et al. 2008). A community can take steps to ensure that water resources are not damaged (e.g., protecting groundwater recharge areas from inappropriate development) and can develop and secure sustainable long-term sources of drinking water. Increasingly, cities and communities are exploring ways to recycle and reuse water and are developing integrated water management systems that take a comprehensive view of water (wastewater, stormwater, surface water, and groundwater).

Food has emerged as a significant concern in community planning, with support for more local and regional food production systems and more concern on the part of consumers about where their food comes from, its healthiness, and the environmental impacts associated with its production and consumption. This extends planning's long-standing concern about the loss of farmland to include preservation and conservation of viable nonrural agricultural communities and production areas, known as "periurban" agriculture. There also is a growing emphasis on urban agriculture, recognizing that cities can be places where large amounts of food production can occur and responding to the desire of many urbanites to grow at least some of their own food. Urban zoning codes have been revised to allow the raising of chickens and other livestock, beekeeping (e.g., recent code changes in New York City), and commercial farming (e.g., recent proposals in Detroit). Cities are engaging in comprehensive community food analyses and strategies, identifying ways to accommodate and support not only the growing of food locally but also food processing and value-added community food enterprises. Rust Belt cities that have lost much of their population during the last half century, such as Cleveland, are reinventing themselves and taking what were once blighted abandoned properties and converting them into commercial, organic urban agriculture.

The advantages of addressing food systems in community plans are many. Planning a sustainable, more local food system can potentially deliver healthier food produced more cheaply; food produced with fewer pesticides and environmental impacts; food with smaller energy and carbon footprints; a stronger sense of place and deeper place connections; as well as new and important community social relationships.

Energy

Despite rapid recent growth in the development of renewable energy sources, nonrenewable sources still account for a full 92 percent of U.S. energy consumption—and this figure is forecast to change very little (to 87 percent) by 2035 (Figure 3.1). This is because renewable energy sources are limited in their overall substitutability for fossil fuels due to their lower "energy returned on energy invested," difficulty of storage, and other factors (Fridley 2010). Our communities will clearly be dependent on nonrenewables for many decades to come unless there is a major shift away from the use of fossil fuels.

Meanwhile, the availability and price of nonrenewable energy sources in the next 25 years will look very different than they did over the previous 25 years. The days of cheap oil are widely recognized to be over (IEA 2010);

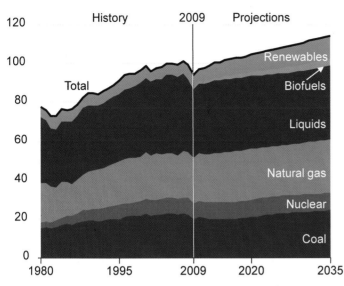

Figure 3.1. U.S. energy use by fuel, 1980–2035, primary energy consumption (quadrillion Btu / year)

Source: U.S. Energy Information Administration, Annual Energy Outlook 2011 Early Release, April 2011, Figure 57.

every year, steadily increasing global demand must be met with oil that is increasingly expensive to discover and produce. Coal supplies are abundant in the United States, but increasing demand from China, together with federal regulations to restrict GHG emissions, may significantly constrain this energy source in the future (Heinberg and Fridley 2010). Natural gas is currently a favored solution for domestic, less-carbon-emitting energy, but there are many unresolved questions about the economic, health, and environmental costs of "unconventional" natural gas—the difficult- or expensive-to-extract gas that is increasingly making up U.S. reserves (http://naturalgas.org/overview/unconvent_ng_resource.asp). Nuclear energy technology has advanced considerably in the last few decades, but complications with insurance, high up-front costs, and waste disposal will likely prevent it from ever providing more than a small fraction of U.S. energy.

We need energy of many types for our communities to function: electricity for homes and businesses, natural gas and oil for heating, and, most significantly, gasoline and diesel fuel for the transportation of people and goods. Most communities and their supporting infrastructure have been built over the last 60 years to run on affordable and abundant fossil fuels. Because energy prices and our energy mix will be changing significantly over the next 25 years and beyond—and will affect economic activity, transportation, land use, and other urban patterns in ways that are difficult to predict—communities need to plan not so much for energy scarcity as for energy uncertainty (Lerch 2007).

Planning for sustaining places can build community energy resilience by:

- encouraging the diversification of local and regional energy sources, such as through the development and use of renewable energy where most applicable;

- investing in highly efficient and "smart" energy technology where appropriate;

- encouraging reduced per capita consumption of energy in general (and energy from nonrenewable sources in particular), both directly and indirectly, such as by integrating energy resilience considerations in decisions about infrastructure and urban patterns and educating the public about conservation practices; and

- reducing energy consumption in new building stock and retrofitting existing building stock.

Large power plants are beyond the jurisdiction of most communities, but most communities can take advantage of those renewable energy technologies that lend themselves to local and distributed installations: solar, wind, biomass, and geothermal, among others.

The new model of distributed renewable energy suggests that cities and communities represent not only places of consumption but also venues for production, and that every community could produce energy. Advancements in smart grids, smart meters, and grid informational technology make the collaborative sharing of small amounts of energy in a community possible. Buildings are increasingly designed to function as small power plants, and plus-energy homes and positive-energy buildings are becoming more common. In European cites, energy-efficient, decentralized combined heat and power (CHP) systems, as well as district heating and cooling systems, are common. Community planning plays an important part in identifying places where such renewable energy can be produced (e.g., Danish plans require designation of areas appropriate for wind production) and in ensuring that undue regulatory obstacles do not exist (e.g., modifying zoning ordinances and development codes to allow installation of solar panels, microturbines, green roofs, etc.).

Climate Change, Natural Disasters, and Community Resilience

One of the largest opportunities in planning today is the integration of climate and sustainability initiatives with the comprehensive planning process. Comprehensive plans benefit greatly from the holistic approach required when creating sustainability and climate plans. Indeed, the comprehensive plan of the near past is outdated in its topics, focus, and structure. A well-executed comprehensive planning effort that includes sustainability goals as well as predisaster mitigation should not only dramatically improve the quality of life in a community but also drastically reduce long-term fiscal maintenance and operational costs due to repeated disaster-recovery episodes (Godschalk et al. 2009).

Cities will play a critical role both in reducing GHG emissions ("mitigation") and in adapting to the impacts of climate change. Creating compact, walkable communities and investing in transit, bicycling, and pedestrian infrastructure will help reduce GHG emissions, as will other efforts such as green building standards, which are aimed at minimizing environmental impacts, reducing long-term costs, and reducing energy consumed by the built environment. Adaptation efforts will include assessing community risk from changes in regional freshwater availability, extreme weather events (e.g., heat waves), rising sea levels, and even changes in economically important environmental systems (e.g., shifting agricultural zones and habitat ranges).

Even if GHG emissions were stabilized today, cities and communities would still face a host of serious impacts and shocks associated with irreversible global average temperature increases. Many of these will present special challenges for certain communities. Climate change will also exacerbate

other environmental problems. Evidence suggests, for instance, that East Coast summer temperature highs will rise significantly, further worsening the existing air-quality problems in cities there.

As much of the U.S. population is in coastal areas (as are many of the world's rapidly urbanizing cities), planning for adaptation and response to long-term sea-level rise is an especially difficult challenge—but it is one that local and regional plans in the United States must begin to tackle. One recent study even suggests that a two-meter sea-level rise should be reflected in the minimum planning standard, though previous estimates had been less than one meter (Pilkey and Young 2009). Even this will be a difficult task for coastal communities, but the comprehensive plan represents an especially appropriate tool for developing and implementing a long-term strategy for retreat from and adaptation to sea-level rise, given the implications for land use and infrastructure.

Planning must also address the range of potential natural hazards and forces that exist in a particular area. Community planning can help to make cities and communities resilient in the long run to these hazards, including earthquakes, hurricanes and coastal storms, riverine flooding, and wildfires. Plans should incorporate detailed mapping of the most dangerous locations and envision land-use patterns that seek to avoid these hazards. Cities can also do much to enhance preparedness on the part of the community and foster greater social resilience by creating physical designs and urban forms that encourage a more vibrant and active social life and help to bolster social networks, as well as support a robust network of community groups, organizations, and clubs that will aid in responding to disasters and other shocks.

Economic Sustainability

A key principle of planning for sustaining places is the resilient economy principle. Many American communities face severe shocks when the U.S. economy and its housing and jobs markets falter. Neighborhood stability is threatened, government budgets shrink because of reductions in real estate– and sales-tax collection, and massive housing foreclosures invite vandalism and crime. Some once-thriving cities face permanent declines in their populations.

Comprehensive plans can be rallying points for analyzing and responding to economic threats. By diversifying their economies and continuing to strengthen their job training, workforce housing, employment centers, and social service bases, growing communities can maintain their economic vitality. By acknowledging the reality of changes in their economic bases, declining communities can craft new strategies fitted to their smaller ecological footprints. (For an explanation of the concept "ecological footprint," see Hancock 2008.)

While the economy is global, and cities and regions cannot influence fundamental economic factors, such as capital markets or foreign costs of production, cities and regions can influence how they position themselves in the global economy by providing the land-use and physical capacity for business growth, locations for catalytic R and D institutions, efficient high-quality infrastructure at an affordable cost, a trained labor force, and the market image of its place, including a reputation for sustainable practices.

Youngstown, Ohio, is an example of a place that developed a plan to respond to the reality of losing its traditional economic base and the ensuing loss of jobs and population. The Youngstown 2010 Plan provides for a city that is "smaller, greener, and cleaner" (www.cityofyoungstownoh .com/about_youngstown/youngstown_2010/plan/plan.aspx; see also the chapter on Youngstown in Faga 2006). Winner of the APA 2007 Award

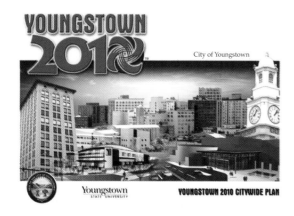

City of Youngstown

YOUNGSTOWN 2010 CITYWIDE PLAN

for Public Outreach, Youngstown involved its leaders and its citizens in a wide-reaching process to ask what should be done now that the steel mills have left. Rather than trying to get back to their previous size, they decided to let go of the past and transform themselves into a good midsized city. Working with Youngstown State University, they built consensus for a new comprehensive plan and for actions, such as creating a business incubator to nurture start-up tech companies. Green job development can be an important component of a sustaining places strategy.

Comprehensive plans can strengthen resilience in other ways as well. In an era of declining global oil supplies, those communities with land-use and infrastructure commitments that provide alternatives to dependence on automobiles will be much more resilient. Similarly, communities that have invested in local food production may be less subject to the global food disruptions and price increases that some predict for the future (Brown 2009).

Susan Wachter's study of Philadelphia's urban greening strategy found that it provided measurable economic benefits, including increases in real estate values (www.pennsylvaniahorticulturalsociety.org/phlgreen/seeing green.htm). Her study of a greened neighborhood found significant increases in the value of individual homes near cleaned lots, street trees, and parks. It also found a considerable increase in the total value of property in those particular communities.

Generally speaking, there are demonstrable economic benefits from all of the sustainability measures and strategies that cities and communities can adopt. Elements of a city or region's green infrastructure deliver benefits that carry considerable economic value and are often much more cost-effective than conventional approaches (e.g., preserving wetlands as a stormwater and flood management option compared with flood-control dams and other expensive engineered approaches). Developers, consumers, and governments may not realize these economic trade-offs unless the full cost of alternative infrastructure approaches is directly linked to the sources of demand through user fees and impact fees. Moving toward sustainability, moreover, will enhance livability and serve to strengthen the economic competiveness of a city or community.

Some cities, businesses, and universities see an economic development opportunity within the movement toward sustainability, positioning their region for new "clean-tech" industry clusters. Some of these cities, such as San Diego, have economic prosperity elements in their comprehensive plans with supportive policies related to these emerging green industries. According to a 2011 Brookings Institution study, both Albany, New York, and Cleveland, Ohio, whose plans are reviewed in this report, are leaders in the development of green jobs (www.brookings.edu/reports/2011/0713_clean_economy.aspx; and www.npr.org/2011/09/02/140131957/surprising-areas-see-growth-in-green-jobs).

Green Infrastructure, Natural Systems

Cities not only alter natural systems and environments but also offer opportunities to protect, conserve, and restore natural resources, as well as to integrate them into urban development patterns. These "green infrastructure" systems are as essential as more traditional forms of urban infrastructure. They provide ecological services and benefits to residents and are major determinants of livability and quality of life in a community—important factors for attracting and retaining the essential talent for emerging green industries. Green elements and infrastructure exist at all scales, from the building to the regional or bioregional. This continuum is sometimes described as "rooftop to region" or even "room to region," suggesting that communities and community plans must work to provide for a coherent, connected green network of ecologically intact parks, forests, habitats, and other natural features. At the regional or citywide scale are larger ecological systems, including wetlands and river systems, aquifers and watersheds, and larger patterns of woodlands and natural lands. These systems are the ecological backbone and framework for community planning, and they provide opportunities for trails, larger parks, and common spaces. At the other end of the geographical scale are the building and neighborhood green elements, from community gardens to street trees, urban forests, green rooftops, and vertical gardens. These features help to address the urban heat island effect, reduce energy consumption and carbon emissions, improve urban air quality, and enhance quality of life.

Trees and urban forests offer environmental and economic value and provide a range of essential services to a city and region, including moderating air pollution, retaining stormwater, shading and cooling urban environments through evapotranspiration, and providing habitat for birds and other wildlife. (See PAS Report no. 555, *Planning the Urban Forest*.) American Forests has been a strong advocate for urban forests and sets the goal of a minimum forest-canopy coverage of 40 percent over an entire metropolitan region. Most American urban areas fail to meet that standard, and in many places the urban forest is in decline. Arid environments, such as cities in the southwest, might achieve these benefits through other landscape strategies.

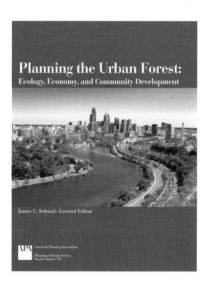

Like many other green features, evidence suggests that the market recognizes an economic premium for homes and neighborhoods that are green. The presence of trees and greenery and convenient access to parks serve to raise the value of private property, as well as deliver extensive public benefits. Providing this green character through the maintenance of natural landscapes, as compared with manufactured gardens, reduces both costs and environmental impacts.

Green infrastructure also has an important role to play in addressing the problems of distressed neighborhoods and minority and low-income populations that too often bear a disproportionate burden of environmental and health hazards. The benefits urban green infrastructure can provide such communities include better air and water quality, improved public health, enhanced aesthetics and safety, "green collar" job opportunities, and local food production (Dunn 2010).

Some now argue for the importance of biophilic cities and communities—places that recognize the importance of daily contact with the natural world. A growing body of literature and research shows that access to nature is essential for a happy, healthy, and productive life (Beatley 2010). Evidence indicates that exposure to nature may help us to be more generous human beings. Exactly what constitutes a biophilic community remains debatable, but local comprehensive plans offer the best hope for envisioning an integrated network of green spaces, parks, trails, habitat systems, and other green features.

Many cities have taken the lead in restoring ecological systems and elements. For example, cities such as Los Angeles and Seoul, South Korea, have adopted ambitious visions for restoring river systems (the Los Angeles River in the former case, the Cheonggyecheon in the latter). As a further example, the community master plan of Oslo, Norway, states the ambitious goal of daylighting (i.e., bringing back to the surface) the seven rivers that traverse the city but are currently in pipes underground (in addition to the Akerselva, which is largely already restored and natural). The City of San Diego has the Multiple Species Conservation Program (MSCP) Plan, which preserves almost 50,000 acres of habitat lands connected to river valleys and canyons, integrated with the city, linked to a regional Multi-Habitat Planning Area. Comprehensive plans can set the stage for major ecological renovation and conservation, establish a long-term template and vision for bringing nature back to urban and metropolitan areas, and profoundly improve the quality of urban life in the process.

In recent years, the ways in which children are increasingly isolated from nature has become a concern. With a significant number of hours spent with computers and electronic media of various kinds, growing up today is unfortunately too often a largely sedentary, indoor experience. Richard Louv, in his 2005 book *Last Child in the Woods,* has challenged us to develop strategies and to make a commitment to tackle what he calls "nature deficit disorder"; community plans can and should increasingly aspire to create the physical conditions for raising "free-range kids," for making it possible for children and families to walk and spend time outside, and for exploring, learning about, and ultimately caring about the environment.

Community Health

Community plans have tremendous implications for influencing the health of Americans. Concern about rising obesity rates and the sedentary and increasingly unhealthy lives and lifestyles of many Americans is evident everywhere. Sprawl can make us sick, providing further support for planning that encourages more compact, walkable neighborhoods and environments. Community plans that address community food systems, as a further example, have the potential to expand access to healthy, nutritious local food, again delivering long-term community health benefits (see, e.g., the Homegrown Minneapolis program at www.ci.minneapolis.mn.us/dhfs/homegrown-home.asp).

National Cooperative Grocers Association

Applying the healthy community principle in preparing a comprehensive plan can identify opportunities for greening neighborhoods. Community gardens can replace abandoned structures. Accessible grocery stores can improve the diets of residents in areas formerly served only by fast-food outlets. Local agriculture and farmers markets can bring fresh foods as well as green jobs (see, e.g., the 2011 Minneapolis Urban Agriculture Policy Plan at www.ci.minneapolis.mn.us/cped/urban_ag_plan.asp). Community centers and parks can enhance recreation opportunities.

Cities can undertake a host of planning actions to enhance community health—social, economic, environmental—and comprehensive plans can play a key role. Communities can build healthy social capital through fostering a sense of community, inviting community engagement and volunteering, and providing ample opportunities for citizens and community groups to be closely involved in the planning process. For example, Vancouver, British Columbia, has adopted a policy on social sustainability that defines two levels—the individual or human capacity and the social or community capacity—and identifies three types of needs: (1) basic needs, such as housing and income; (2) individual needs for learning and self-development; and (3) community needs for development of networks and social interaction (http://vancouver.ca/sustainability/documents/social_sus_p1.pdf).

The need for a new approach to comprehensive planning is clear. Thanks to the sustainability challenges of the 21st century, comprehensive planning is at a watershed moment in its evolution. The next chapter takes up the role and status of the comprehensive plan in addressing sustainability.

CHAPTER 4

The Role and Status of the
Comprehensive Plan in Sustaining Places

Why single out the comprehensive plan as the tool of choice to deal with the sustainability challenges of this century? The plan has the legal authority to act as the vehicle for guiding community development, the scope to cover the necessary functions and facilities, and the history of practice to inspire public acceptance of its policies.

The plan is also the ideal vehicle to address the principles of planning for sustaining places. Comprehensive by definition, the role of the plan is to look across all of the structures and forces that determine a community's future well-being and to intervene strategically in those processes that determine whether the community will be sustainable, as measured in terms of its environment, economy, and equity. Of all the tools for influencing the future available to communities, the comprehensive plan is the only one with a mandate to set communitywide goals, to develop processes for engaging citizens in determining and monitoring goal achievement, and to assign responsibilities and priorities for implementing its proposals.

The comprehensive plan can provide social and economic benefits through its role as the repository of the community consensus about its desired future and how to achieve it. By communicating the community's development values, the plan informs developers about the preferred types of development and the rules of the game to be followed, minimizing their risks and minimizing the risk to the public concerning the outcomes. By informing local businesses and organizations about land-use and public facilities development, the plan makes their operations more efficient. By serving as the public statement of community growth priorities, the plan facilitates collaboration among public and nongovernmental agencies, increasing their ability to contribute to the overall public welfare.

THE POWER AND SCOPE OF THE COMPREHENSIVE PLAN

In the United States, the practice of comprehensive planning varies from state to state. The comprehensive plan goes under a variety of names that reflect local conventions, such as the "master plan" in New Jersey, the "general plan" in California, or the "plan of conservation and development" in Connecticut. In spite of these differences, the comprehensive plan is typically distinguished from other types of plans by the following characteristics:

- *Geographic coverage.* The plan's unit of geography is typically the jurisdiction or political unit, such as a town, city, county, or province, because both the adoption of the plan (conferring its legal status) and its implementation (through ordinances, capital budgeting, and discretionary decisions) fall to an elected governing body. Where regional comprehensive plans are adopted, they are most successful where an institutionalized framework for regional coordination exists and is effective, such as a Council of Governments (COG).

- *Long-range perspective.* The time horizon for the plan is typically two decades or more, reflecting both the demographic and economic projections on which the plan is based and the time needed to implement its policies and actions. Plans may provide capacity for, as well as influence, much longer periods, but it is wise to comprehensively update plans periodically due to changing circumstances and values in each generation.

- *Community vision.* The plan typically starts with a big-picture vision for the future of the community, based on a public outreach effort. The specific policies and actions in the plan flow from and support that vision.

- *Policy focus.* Plan content tends to emphasize policy guidance due to the plan's long-term focus and the role it fulfills in providing the policy basis for land use and other regulations. However, most plans contain a mix of policy and action, and the implementation element is becoming an increasingly important plan component.

- *Integrated systems.* The comprehensive plan addresses physical, transportation, economic, environmental, and social systems that make up a jurisdiction and enable it to pursue its desired future vision. While most traditional comprehensive plans retain a particular focus on land use due to the historic connection between planning and zoning, they link land-use policy to these other systems. The plan is the one public document that looks at these varied systems in their totality so that as a group they are internally consistent.

The comprehensive plan also has legal standing that gives it prominence among planning and policy documents. Its status is established by enabling legislation and case law. It is the basis for zoning regulations; the foundation for capital improvements, urban design, and other land-use and environmental regulations; and a potential guide for economic, social, and cultural aspirations.

The comprehensive plan seeks to shape both public- and private-sector investment and, therefore, has three primary vectors of implementation. The first is to serve as the policy foundation for development and environmental regulations, including zoning. The second is to provide guidance for discretionary decisions, such as petitions to amend the zoning map or special use permits. The third is to guide public capital investments, such as roadways, transit, water and wastewater systems, parks, and schools. Coordinating these major public investments—each with long lead times, extended life spans, and high costs—with private development is what makes comprehensive planning relevant.

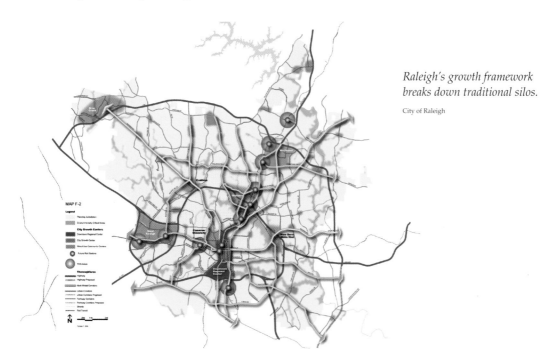

Raleigh's growth framework breaks down traditional silos.

City of Raleigh

The legal status of comprehensive plans varies across states and nations. In the United States, most states started with the 1920s-era Standard State Enabling Acts for planning and zoning, which stated that zoning districts "should be drawn in accordance with a Comprehensive Plan." Today, states vary from those with no requirements for comprehensive planning to those that mandate comprehensive plan content (California, Florida, New Jersey, and others). The lack of common state-level guidelines and mandates has opened the door for innovation from creative local governments. However, state guidelines and mandates generally lead to a broader and more consistent approach to planning.

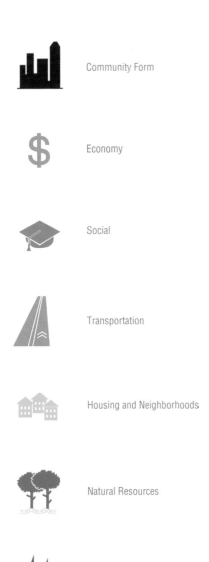

Figure 4.1. The eight interrelated systems in the Albany, New York, 2030 Comprehensive Plan

City of Albany

While the scope of comprehensive planning continues to expand and evolve, the traditional focus on land-use patterns as they relate to other systems remains a critical part of the solution to major sustainability problems, including greenhouse gas (GHG) emissions, water shortages, and habitat loss. How land use affects sustainability is the subject of a growing body of research (see, e.g., Ewing et al. 2007). Furthermore, the breadth of subject matters covered by the comprehensive plan provides the opportunity for an integrated systems approach to replace the traditional "silo" model.

COMMUNITIES AS SYSTEMS

Systems thinking is an effective way to move beyond traditional planning models. While commonly used by businesses to achieve outcomes, such as increased profitability or (pertinent to sustainability) reduced waste or energy use, this approach has rarely been applied systematically to cities and regions, largely because of their levels of complexity, including political and decision-making complexity. However, the basic notions of systems thinking are well suited to comprehensive planning, particularly to overcome the silo approach resulting from preparing related plan elements, such as land use and transportation, separately.

A systems approach organizes the elements of the plan to work together if the vision statement is to be realized (i.e., "the whole is greater than the sum of the parts"). Here, an effective plan aligns systems across geographic scales (neighborhood, city, region, and beyond) and plan functions (e.g., community form, mobility, green infrastructure) to focus on the connections between plan components. The opportunity exists for an even more robust application of system concepts in comprehensive plan development and implementation. For example, the Albany, New York, 2030 Comprehensive Plan takes a systems approach that organizes the plan into eight interdependent systems defined by their subject areas or functions (e.g., community form, transportation, housing and neighborhoods, and institutions). Five system principles inform developers of the overarching direction set by citizens (expressed in the vision statement based on public input) into strategies, actions, and priorities for implementation:

1. Target interconnections (overlaps and leverage points) between system components (i.e., strategies and actions) to influence system behavior in the desired direction.

2. Build feedback loops that generate momentum for positive change.

3. Increase system resilience (i.e., the ability to recover from or adapt to disturbance or change).

4. Create synergies between different levels of the system hierarchy (e.g., site, neighborhood, city, region, and beyond).

5. Use an adaptive management process to implement the plan.

Systems thinking can suggest innovative ways to integrate plan components and to apply planning principles for sustaining places. By visualizing the community as an integrated system of environment, economy, and equity, the trade-offs between alternative planning proposals can be illustrated. Diagramming the relationships among participation, implementation, and regionalism can suggest new ways to build effective social capital. A systems view of the community and its elements lends itself to developing and implementing sustainability metrics.

Systems thinking can also identify opportunities for cross-integration between the comprehensive plan and other community plans and policies. The comprehensive plan should influence, and be influenced by, plans and programs for sustainable development, hazard mitigation, economic devel-

Albany, New York

WRT

opment, affordable housing, utility extensions, public facilities, annexation, transfer of development rights, agriculture, public transportation, capital investment, and other community development and infrastructure policies. The comprehensive plan should be at the center of a local government's sustainability vision and actions. Thus, sustainable community planners must expressly identify and connect with related plans developed to comply with state or federal programs, as well as those developed by local government and nonprofit agencies. Coordination should be both vertical and horizontal.

INCORPORATING SUSTAINABILITY INTO THE PLANNING PROCESS

Legislation enabling comprehensive plans often provides minimal direction on the plan-making process. Typically, a local government must provide opportunities for public participation and hold a formal public hearing to adopt the plan, which will include elements addressing standard topics, such as land use, infrastructure, and transportation. In order to produce plans that address broad sustainability principles, each step of the planning process should highlight sustainability as a primary goal, and a more inclusive and systematic participation process is needed to help the community understand how the systems interact.

For example, the 2007 Marin Countywide Plan addresses climate change and other sustainable development issues, in addition to the legally required elements. It establishes the long-term goal of reducing the county's GHG footprint by at least half, to a level similar to that of Western European countries. To achieve its goal, the plan was reformatted to address three main topics: nature, the built environment, and people. In the Marin plan, the Natural Systems and Agriculture element deals with related topics, such as biological and water resources, environmental hazards, air pollution and GHGs, open space and trails, and ranching, farming, and food. The Built Environment element deals with energy, mineral resources, housing, transportation, and public facilities and services. The Socioeconomic element deals with child care, safety, diversity, education, environmental injustice, public health, arts and culture, historic and archaeological resources, and parks and recreation. Each element includes metrics to measure the success of the goals and policies and asks the questions: What are the desired outcomes? Why is this important? How will results be achieved? How will success be measured?

Answers to these questions are organized into goals, policies, implementation programs, and a series of indicators, benchmarks, and targets. By translating the technical plan aspects into clear and easily understood questions with measurable answers, the plan made clear its rationale to the public. By the time the Marin County Board of Supervisors unanimously adopted the plan, 115 public meetings involving some 2,000 participants had been held.

The Marin framework for sustainability rests on a base of natural systems, over which are layered agriculture, built environment, socioeconomic capital, and community well-being (Figure 4.2).

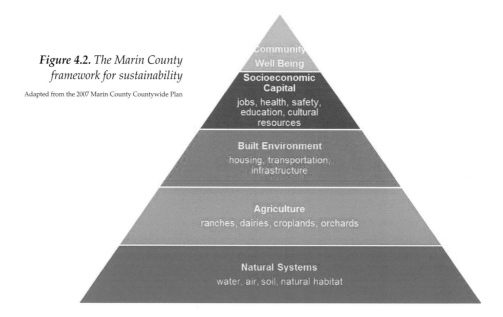

Figure 4.2. *The Marin County framework for sustainability*

Adapted from the 2007 Marin County Countywide Plan

Community Well Being

Socioeconomic Capital
jobs, health, safety, education, cultural resources

Built Environment
housing, transportation, infrastructure

Agriculture
ranches, dairies, croplands, orchards

Natural Systems
water, air, soil, natural habitat

The 2009 Minneapolis Plan represents a more traditional approach in terms of plan format for sustainable growth (www.ci.minneapolis.mn.us/cped/comp_plan_update_draft_plan.asp). While it contains a central focus on sustainability, the plan is organized into the familiar elements of land use, transportation, housing, economic development, and the like. However, it follows the other characteristics of planning for sustainable places. For example, its strong implementation section is consistent with the region's 2030 Regional Development Framework; conforms with policy plans for transportation, water resources, and parks; is compatible with school district plans; and provides a framework for neighborhood and area master plans, corridor plans, housing plans, and public works plans. Implementation responsibilities are assigned to specific departments and agencies, and plan implementation is tied to development regulations, capital improvement plans, and other policy tools.

The approaches of the Marin and Minneapolis plans, as well as the other plans reviewed for this report, when translated into more general terms, suggest a series of steps to follow in planning for sustaining places. Every one of these plans sprang from a community commitment to sustainability, developed its own vision of sustainability based on local conditions, and implemented its vision through goals, policies, and actions whose effectiveness was measured and publicly reported.

Step 1: Commit to a Process for Creating a Plan for Sustaining Places

The governing body needs to champion sustainability, provide adequate funding, and give direction to the planning effort. This commitment to address social, economic, and environmental components of sustainability sets the stage for sustainable outcomes, including the plan, planning roles, and the planning process.

- *The comprehensive plan* should guide decision making and should be based on a shared vision, standards, and directions emerging from public discussion of choices and consequences. The vision and directions become the context for preparing detailed communitywide policies and area plans.

- *Planning roles* should provide for broad stakeholder engagement and interdepartmental involvement in plan preparation to ensure that civic responsibilities are addressed, public understanding and support is created, and organizational buy-in for plan implementation is developed.

- *The planning process* should systematically identify sustainability issues, assemble options for action, and consider the choices and consequences of actions as a basis for plan adoption and implementation.

A robust public engagement program that reaches out to all segments of the community, including underserved populations and others who do not traditionally participate in planning, is key to the process for planning for sustaining places. A variety of methods can be used, ranging from digital technology (social media, interactive web technology, keypad polling, etc.) to getting out into the community to meet people on their own turf (as opposed to expecting them to come to meetings). The goal is to involve not just already engaged stakeholders but also representatives of the community as a whole in defining the issues important to them, articulating a vision for a sustainable future, and setting priorities for implementation.

Step 2: Forge a Vision of Sustainability

Technical analysis needs to be combined with stakeholder participation in order to identify sustainability issues and alternative ways to solve sustainability problems. Organizing information around tenets of sustainability introduces sustainability principles and invites a broad and integrated consideration of topics. One useful technique is to spell out potential future scenarios as a means of organizing options for public discussion. Scenarios help participants realize that the future is not fixed and can be shaped by personal and public decisions. Each scenario should be solidly based on available evidence about consequences for sustainability and on feasible funding strategies. Analytical models can assist in considering the "what if" consequences of particular scenarios.

The goal should be to develop a vision of local sustainability broadly supported by the community (see, e.g., the 2008 Eco City Charter of the City of Alexandria, Virginia, at http://alexandriava.gov/Eco-City). The visioning process invites the public, including businesses, residents, and local organizations, to identify and test alternative urban development paths, and to measure the environmental, economic, and fiscal implications of each path. Preparing a description of a desired future vision provides a way to think comprehensively about the shape of a city, services, and funding necessary to address both local and broader issues. For example, the Sustainable Sydney 2030 Plan is based on a vision for a green, global, and connected city that was developed during an 18-month consultation with citizens (www.sydney2030.com.au), and the Vancouver, British Columbia, CityPlan process engaged more than 100,000 people in a scenario-based public process (http://vancouver.ca/commsvcs/planning/cityplan/cityplan.htm). The City of San Diego began with a two-year strategic framework visioning process with the public that resulted in the City of Villages concept, prior to beginning its work on updating its general plan.

Step 3: Develop Objectives, Policies, and Actions to Implement the Vision

To carry out the proposed vision, the planning process should identify a comprehensive strategy linking goals, objectives, policies, and actions. These will vary depending on the community's resources, needs, and capacities. However, certain elements are important, including a broad base of public support, a schedule of tasks and priorities, a set of measurable indicators, and a process for monitoring and revising the plan as necessary in light of changing conditions.

THE CONTENT OF THE PLAN

Following the model set by most state enabling legislation for comprehensive plans, the traditional comprehensive plan is organized into individual elements that address discrete planning topics or functions. Pennsylvania, for example, requires all comprehensive plans to deal with land use, housing, movement of people and goods (transportation), community facilities and services, natural and historic resource protection, and water supply, and it specifies additional requirements for county comprehensive plans. California law mandates that seven elements be addressed in general plans—land use, open space, conservation, housing, circulation, noise, and safety—plus any other elements that the legislative body of the county or city wishes to adopt, although jurisdictions have flexibility as to how to present those elements.

The obvious drawback of this traditional model is that it can potentially lead jurisdictions to deal with related areas, such as land use, transportation, and utilities, in isolation, particularly when the elements are prepared separately by staff or consultants with different missions and technical expertise. However, state mandates for internal consistency and sustainability targets can force local jurisdictions to address the interrelationships of the different elements with the aim of achieving a goal, such as GHG emission targets under Assembly Bill 32 (AB32) in California.

Some local governments are following a new model that integrates separate functional elements into coordinated plan sections and broadens the scope of elements considered. New topics address contemporary issues, such as energy planning, GHG emissions, climate change adaptation, hazard mitigation, affordable housing, access to jobs services for underserved members of the community, and others. These comprehensive plans also include a vision statement developed through community input in the planning process and depict the desired community future during the time horizon of the plan (typically 20 years and beyond). By setting an overall direction for the specific policies and strategies contained in the plan elements, the vision statement becomes an important driver in the integration of plan elements.

Breaking the mold of the traditional comprehensive plan's discrete elements by developing more inclusive themes or topics offers opportunities for integrating functional elements into the plan. An early example is the FOCUS Kansas City (Missouri) Comprehensive Plan, which received APA's Outstanding Planning Award for a Plan in 1999. Phase 1 of the planning process established a vision statement and 14 major themes and statements of policies to achieve the vision. The full strategic and comprehensive plan prepared in Phase 2 consisted of seven action plans, ranging from a Citywide Physical Framework Plan and Neighborhood Prototypes Plan to subarea plans (Downtown Core and Northlands) and functional plans (Preservation, Human Investment, and Governance). Twelve key strategies or "building blocks" (e.g., FOCUS Centers, Connecting Corridors, and Moving about the City) were interwoven throughout the seven plans.

A more recent example is Plan Cheyenne (Wyoming), which won APA's 2007 Daniel Burnham Award for a Comprehensive Plan. Plan Cheyenne's basic organization consists of three integrated plan components—Community Plan, Parks and Recreation Master Plan, and Transportation Master Plan—and four Building Blocks: Snapshot, Structure, Shape, and Build (www.planchey enne.com/pdf/final/1/Cheyenne_exec_summ_Final_Apr07.pdf).

- *Snapshot* captures the existing conditions of the community.

- *Structure* is the form-giving and design-based part of the plan.

- *Shape* establishes values and principles for how and where the community should grow in the future.

- *Build* establishes strategies to implement the plan.

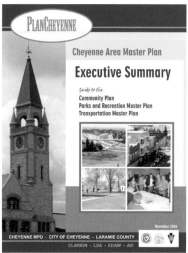

Cheyenne MPO

Clearly, the comprehensive plan is an effective vehicle for sustaining places. However, plans are prepared at many geographic scales and differ in their ability to affect sustainability, depending on their scale. The next chapter takes up the topic of planning scale and sustainability.

CHAPTER 5

Planning Scale and the
Vertical Integration of Plans

 The territory covered by a plan determines the extent to which a plan can create sustainable places comprehensively. A planning challenge is finding the right scale at which to work with the environmental, social, and economic systems that sustain our communities. For example, watersheds, habitat systems, transportation networks, and job and housing markets usually operate at the regional level, whereas many policies and day-to-day decisions that influence demand for resources and services are local.

Complicating matters is the fact that political boundaries often have little relationship to the geography and size of those environmental, social, and economic systems, combined with the historic weakness of regional planning in the United States. The challenge is to overcome this historic weakness and to breathe new life into regional planning. The responsible regionalism principle seeks to answer this challenge by explicitly tying community sustainability to the sustainability of the larger region.

Typically, the scale of a comprehensive plan is associated with a jurisdiction's boundaries, coinciding with the political and legal powers for implementation, especially locally controlled land use. However, such a man-made scale more often than not has little relationship to the scale associated with the sustainable use of resources.

Air quality and GHG emissions are a function of commuting patterns and transportation networks designed to take people from where they live to where they work, shop, socialize, and recreate. Given that most metropolitan areas are a combination of bedroom communities and job centers that make up an interdependent regional economy, planning for individual jurisdictions alone cannot adequately address GHG emissions attributable to transportation.

© iStockphoto.com/EdStock

Water management involves watersheds and engineered conveyance systems well beyond the scope of most local jurisdictions. While local conservation and reclamation is the most sustainable approach, water that naturally feeds into the local aquifer often come from distant sources. The great viaduct systems of the southwestern United States cross not just local boundaries but state lines; 80 percent of the San Diego region's water comes from other areas (SDCWA n.d.). Moreover, sustainable use of water is not just a water issue; it is also an energy issue since the transport of water across mountains and deserts uses significant amounts of energy.

Habitat systems are intended for the ecological area needed to sustain different plant and animal species. While they may be small and within a jurisdiction for some species, they are often large and regional, depending on the species' territorial and biodiversity needs.

Electricity can be generated locally, sometimes even within a single development or community with distributed systems. But in the United States, most power is generated within a regional grid network extending beyond state boundaries and driven mostly by the costs of fuel, production, and conveyance, plus a return to investors, without full accounting for environmental costs.

Economic prosperity ultimately is determined by a region's ability to export goods and services to external markets, bringing dollars into a region that are then distributed locally, as inputs to production are purchased and wages are spent; how economic opportunities are shared among an area's population is the root question of social equity.

While there are examples of super- and interregional plans to address a particular environmental issue, such as water delivery in the southwestern United States, these plans are not comprehensive enough to achieve overall sustainability because they do not have jurisdictional authority that directly influences demand for resources. That authority, as well as the comprehensive plans enabled by that authority, usually comes at the local and intraregional level.

Since planning for sustainable places is done at different geographies and scales, it is done most effectively when the different scales of comprehensive planning come together to reinforce one another.

THE REGIONAL PLAN

The region is the most appropriate scale to comprehensively address sustainability because the resources to be sustained are, at a minimum, regional— whether related to the environment (air, water, and habitat), the economy (labor, jobs, infrastructure, and physical capacity), or social equity (fair housing and access to opportunities). But what regional scale is appropriate? That depends on the resources addressed by the plan and the sources of demand that consume these resources, as well as economic interdependencies, particularly relationships among jobs, housing, and transportation.

Many of the tools for implementing planning policies to create sustaining places—such as land-use laws, infrastructure financing mechanisms, many environmental regulations, and political decisions—are enabled at the state level; in some states they are enabled by home rule or charter city authority, applied at the local jurisdictional level. A local jurisdiction's comprehensive plan and sustainability policies, while important on their own, are more effective when linked to or consistent with a regional plan.

Comprehensive regional plans are usually prepared for regions within a state, such as the Regional Blueprint plans that California councils of government (COGs) prepare. A few examples cross state lines, such as the Tahoe Regional Planning Agency's plan, formed to protect Lake Tahoe's water quality by managing growth and resources in an economic, ecological, and watershed region that includes Nevada and California. Interstate plans, however, are the exception rather than the rule.

Lake Tahoe

© iStockphoto/Mariusz Blach

States can have tremendous influence on the extent to which sustainability is embodied in local and regional comprehensive plans. This influence comes through mandates, performance requirements, incentives, state agency oversight, funding, or some combination thereof.

Some states require regional plans for portions of the state. The California Coastal Act, enacted by voter initiative in the 1970s, established the California Coastal Commission and policies to protect the state's coastal resources. It requires that local coastal plans be prepared in accordance with the act, subject to the commission's approval. Amendments must be approved by, or can be appealed to, the commission. North Carolina has a similar requirement for preparation of land-use plans for its 20 coastal counties under the North Carolina Coastal Area Management Act.

The State of California, under Assembly Bill 32, set targets for reducing GHG emissions to 80 percent of 1990 levels by 2020. A subsequent implementing bill, Senate Bill 375 (SB375), provides for regional COGs to reduce GHG emissions by a target amount set by the California Air Resources Board. COGs are required to prepare Regional Comprehensive Plans with Sustainable Communities Strategies that are coordinated with their Regional Transportation Plans to meet these targets.

New Jersey has a statewide growth management plan that directs growth into existing townships and cities through the use of state transportation dollars and allocation criteria, as well as a transfer of development rights (TDR) program to protect agricultural and open space areas. Maryland has a Smart Growth program that requires counties to designate Priority Funding Areas where growth is encouraged around existing towns and cities by concentrating public investment for new infrastructure, such as roads and schools, in these areas. Its Plan Maryland strategy includes a number of policies designed to encourage sustainable development.

The metropolitan area is the most common scale for regional comprehensive plans. Populations within metropolitan regions share natural resources, such as air, habitat, and water. These areas are also economic regions that share a workforce, housing and job markets, and the transportation, energy, water, and waste infrastructures that support economic activity. The linkage of transportation systems and housing was one of the original reasons for regional coordination and planning through metropolitan planning organizations (MPOs), formed to disseminate federal transportation dollars. Many MPOs have expanded their purview to include open space, habitat, air and water quality, and economic development. Some became COGs, governed by a board comprising representatives of the multiple local jurisdictions within their regions, such as cities, townships, and counties, most of which usually retain land-use authority even when planning is done at a regional level. Although most do not have land-use powers, regional authorities can influence land use, such as the Metropolitan Council of the Minneapolis–St. Paul metropolitan area, which coordinates plans for regional systems with local comprehensive plans.

A regional comprehensive plan, taken together with a regional transportation plan, is the basis for transportation planning and expenditure priorities; therefore, it can have tremendous influence on land-use patterns, vehicle-miles traveled that generate carbon emissions, and access to economic opportunities, even if the plan does not have direct land-use authority. The power of the transportation purse can have as much influence as any land-use regulation because most land uses are of limited value without access to the regional transportation network.

The regional comprehensive plan is also an important document for establishing policies to deter sprawl. The sustainable regional plan works best when regional funding sources are associated with its implementation, such as a regionwide sales tax for transportation infrastructure or a tax-sharing agreement among member jurisdictions. Without a strong regional plan to guide local land-use policies and regional transportation policies, or one with even more authority that requires local plans to be consistent with the regional plan, sustainability efforts and policies of one jurisdiction may be countered by lax policies in another. Self-interested parties may play one jurisdiction off against another. The regional comprehensive plan is the policy vehicle for coordinating the various comprehensive plans of cities, townships, and unincorporated counties. It is the key document for sustaining places, as exemplified in the San Diego regional plan.

A recent federal program to encourage planning for regional sustainability has been initiated by the federal Partnership for Sustainable Communities, which includes the U.S. Department of Housing and Urban Development (HUD), Department of Transportation (DOT), and the Environmental Protection Agency (EPA).[1] The partnership recognizes the importance of vertically integrating plans to achieve sustainability-minded results, beginning with the region. The partnership has established six Livability Principles to coordinate investments and guide policy:

1. Provide more transportation choices.

2. Promote equitable, affordable housing.

3. Enhance economic competitiveness.

4. Support existing communities.

5. Coordinate and leverage federal policies and investment.

6. Value communities and neighborhoods.

Partnership initiatives include a grant program to promote regional planning efforts that integrate housing, transportation, and land-use decision making and increase capacity to achieve economic prosperity, environmental quality, and social equity. Referred to as Regional Plans for Sustainable Development, these efforts must be led by a broad regional coalition of public, private, and nonprofit sector partners; incorporate extensive public participation, with an emphasis on reaching underserved populations; and achieve measurable outcomes, such as:

• reduced social and economic disparities for low-income, minority communities and other disadvantaged populations;

• reduced vehicle-miles traveled (VMT) per capita and transportation-related emissions; and

• reduced overall combined housing and transportation costs per household.

As the lead agency for the Partnership, HUD provided $98 million in 2010 grant funding to 44 regions across the nation to develop new (or implement existing) Regional Plans for Sustainable Development. The grantees ranged from large urban areas (e.g., Chicago and Houston) to smaller metropolitan (e.g., Eugene, Oregon, and Portland, Maine) and rural regions (e.g., Apache County, Arizona, and New River Valley, Virginia). HUD's FY 2011 budget includes $70 million for a second round of Sustainable Communities Regional Planning Grants. Required by HUD to be completed within a three-year timeframe, these efforts will provide fertile testing grounds for developing and implementing regional approaches to sustainability.

THE COUNTY PLAN

In some states, the county plan functions as the regional plan, especially in rural regions. In many states where the county government has land-use authority, that authority is limited to unincorporated areas.

Some counties, such as Montgomery County, Maryland, have taken the position that unincorporated areas should remain agricultural, open space, and very low-density residential, with most development encouraged in cities and towns. However, the relatively low cost of land in unincorporated county areas compared to that in cities creates a strong economic incentive for property owners and developers to convert rural land to suburban residential development, especially when the rural land is within commuting distance of a region's job centers. This economic incentive creates sprawl that facilitates longer driving distances and more vehicle-miles traveled, greater fuel consumption, and more GHG emissions. It can also consume open space areas, diminishing the sustainability of habitat systems, recreation areas, or certain economic sectors, such as agriculture. This economic incentive to "open up the back country" to development is mitigated if a regional plan, especially transportation and water service funding, does not encourage the enabling infrastructure in the first place.

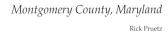

Montgomery County, Maryland

Rick Pruetz

Unless a comprehensive county plan addresses these pressures through land-use policies, infrastructure priorities, and financing systems and is coordinated with a regional plan, a regional sustainability plan cannot be fully effective. The Marin Countywide Plan and the Montgomery County, Maryland, growth policy plan are examples of county plans that directly address such pressures.

THE RURAL PLAN

The benefits of blending sustainability and comprehensive planning are possibly more pronounced in small communities. Small towns and rural communities may prepare rural plans, expressing their sense of independence. Rural residents often are less transient than their big-city counterparts, know their major infrastructure systems, and are familiar with the history of decision making in their communities. The scale of small communities' operating budgets is more accessible. Community members are more likely to understand the amounts of money being allocated to various services.

Union County, Pennsylvania
WRT

While these characteristics apply to both suburban and small rural communities, important differences remain between these two contexts. Suburban communities are tied to their metropolitan areas. Planning for sustainability in these circumstances requires both an internal focus and regional coordination. In rural areas, residents tend to be influenced by the agricultural economy and are more closely attuned to the impacts of climate and the availability of natural resources. Many rural communities suffer from slow but steady outmigration and lack robust economic systems. They are hesitant to take on a comprehensive planning process, and those that do often underestimate the value it can bring. It takes a commitment to overcome the inertia built into "just doing projects" and to take time to think about how to maximize impact and systematically prioritize efforts. Treating planning as a necessary phase of infrastructure investment and a recurring expense can greatly improve long-term performance and avoid the sticker shock that deters smaller communities from fully engaging in the process. The comprehensive plan can help sustain and leverage the lifestyle attributes of rural communities for economic development, such as agriculture and rural tourism.

When rural communities engage in a visionary planning process, true sustainability is often at the heart of the collective vision, given the populations' closeness to the land and resources. It is in working backward from this point, and in helping the community understand the steps toward that goal, that planners can provide the most value.

The trend toward urbanization will continue to strain small communities. In the coming decades there will be a few winners and more losers when it comes to the economic viability of small communities. Proactively choosing to undergo a planning process may be the best tactic to place a small community on a successful path. When comprehensive plans are done well, the community develops a stronger knowledge base about its current state and the strategies that can catalyze a shift in performance and ultimately quality of life. The consensus built through the planning process can be more ubiquitous and recognizable in small communities because it is often possible to literally get those charged with implementing recommendations in one room on a regular basis. When rural communities move quickly to implement the vision and recommendations that come out of a sustainably focused comprehensive plan, they can preserve and enhance their small-town quality of life while simultaneously placing their community on a path toward long-term prosperity.

THE CITY COMPREHENSIVE PLAN

Cities typically have jurisdiction over policies and regulations, in particular land-use policies, which most directly influence demand for resources. Some states, such as California, New Jersey, and Florida, require local jurisdictions to prepare comprehensive plans (called "general plans" in California). In most states, comprehensive plans are not mandated but are enabled and encouraged. Some states require that comprehensive plans address certain elements or topics.

Laws in California and Florida also require that local governments make capital improvement plans consistent with the comprehensive plan; therefore, the comprehensive plan links its sustainability policies with a city's infrastructure plans. These laws provide some consistency among comprehensive plans within the state, which facilitates coordination among different jurisdictions within a region. They also provide the framework for addressing sustainability with policies appropriate for the particular jurisdiction.

While some cities have chosen to have a sustainability element, others structure their comprehensive plan to be the sustainability plan, recognizing the importance of interconnecting policies of the various elements to create sustainable places. Sustainable habitat and open space policies should have corresponding land-use policies where development is allowed. Mobility policies for alternative modes to the car, such as walking, bicycling, and transit, should coordinate with urban design policies for street design and density policies to create a critical mass of demand for these modes. In the City of San Diego's conservation element, a matrix lists policies in other elements related to sustainability, reinforcing the notion that a truly sustainable plan must be comprehensive and holistic, not just topical. The social equity aspect of sustainability, when addressed, is more often within city comprehensive plans, since cities tend to have the most diverse populations, socially, culturally, and economically. Comprehensive plans address issues such as access to jobs, community reinvestment, housing affordability, fair housing, public facilities provision, and environmental justice. While these social equity issues are common in many city comprehensive plans, they are not exclusive to cities.

THE COMMUNITY PLAN

For small jurisdictions, a comprehensive plan usually presents the policies that directly affect what one can do with a specific parcel of land. For large jurisdictions, however, the comprehensive plan is an overarching set of policies focusing on citywide systems, while community or subarea plans are the vehicles for regulating particular properties through policies appropriate to the character of individual communities.

These plans establish the land-use policies for individual parcels that guide the associated regulations and zoning for their development. Specific public facilities, street design, and open space areas are identified at the community level. Urban design and historic preservation are particular to the context. Even social equity and economic development strategies more attuned to a community's socioeconomic characteristics, business opportunities, and competitive advantages can be incorporated.

The community and neighborhood are where sustainability policies are grounded; they are the scale at which the broader regional or city comprehensive plan is implemented, directly influencing demand for the resources to be sustained. The urban form and mixture of land uses that influence transportation choices—walking, bicycling, transit, or driving—are defined and implemented through associated regulations and infrastructure priorities derived from the plan. This is the policy vehicle for coordinating infrastructure, public facilities, and land use, with facilities sized to meet demand and designed to be more efficient and sustainable, perhaps serving multiple purposes, such as "green" or "complete" streets. The plan can identify specific areas vulnerable to the impacts of climate change, such as rising sea levels in coastal communities and opportunities for adaptation; delineate native habitat areas; and propose proactive community development initiatives.

The City of San Diego is structured this way, with a general plan and community plans (technically, components of the general plan) prepared separately but in accordance with it. Updating community plans keeps the general plan fresh, since in any given year, one or more communities are updating their plans and are keeping the general plan in the public eye. It also allows for innovation and experimentation. Concepts, policies, or implementation measures that some communities may resist can be tried in a community willing to experiment. The innovations and lessons learned are then shared with and available to the rest of the city.

The preparation of the community plan involves more direct public participation and input since it is closest to the people and their neighborhoods and quality of life. Often the public takes more interest in the community plan because the decisions can affect not only their neighborhoods and day-to-day quality of life but also their property values. Environmental impacts are immediate, and mitigation, if possible, is particular to the community.

Despite their grassroots immediacy, community plans, even ones focused on sustainability, should be linked and consistent with citywide and regional comprehensive plans. Otherwise, the risk—even temptation—is to protect the immediate environment at the expense of the larger environment. Without this relationship to sustainable policies and goals at a broader geography, a community plan can become a vehicle for intolerance (e.g., by opposing density even when the proposed density is supported by infrastructure and transit and when some additional density is necessary to support a regional transportation system that generates fewer GHG emissions).

THE MASTER PLAN

The master plan guides the development of a specific area, whether a mixed use project, residential subdivision, or a large campus. While a good master plan integrates many planning, design, and development principles, most are not comprehensive at this smaller scale. Instead, they are the tangible component of a broader comprehensive planning system.

Master plans can support goals for sustaining places. Indeed, some of the best examples of planning for sustaining places are at this scale. Master plans can be the planning vehicles that convert policies of large-scale policy plans into actual built projects that people can touch and visit to observe practices that sustain places.

Recently a new kind of master planned development has emerged that makes sustaining places concerns its top priority. Some are known as "eco-villages," which are small communities intentionally designed to be more socially, economically, and environmentally sustainable. These development plans emphasize forms of mobility that generate fewer GHG emissions, such as walking, bicycling, and transit. The land is often used efficiently to save open space and indigenous habitats. Buildings are situated and designed relative to the sun to reduce reliance on mechanical heating and air-conditioning to maintain comfort. They may use recycled materials for insulation and much of their construction. They may be engineered with distributive and passive energy systems, relying on air, sun, and thermal sources for their electricity and heat, which are also shared among the uses within the master plan area. To reduce water consumption, they may incorporate native landscaping and xeriscaping and perhaps reclaimed and naturally captured water. Community gardens may provide locally sourced food. Recognizing this important role, different organizations have developed metrics for identifying sustainable master plans, such as the U.S. Green Building Council's LEED–Neighborhood Development (ND) certification, Greentrip's criteria, or the STAR Community Index under development by ICLEI–Local Governments for Sustainability (Feiden 2011).

THE PLANS COME TOGETHER

Goals for sustaining places are most effectively achieved when the different scales of comprehensive planning come together and reinforce one another, vertically integrating. The regional comprehensive plan provides the framework policies for regional systems, particularly transportation, water, open space, urban boundaries, and the economy, consistent with the geography of the resources to be sustained and economic relationships. Regional comprehensive plans have associated regional transportation plans that guide capital budgeting for regional transportation improvements. Taken together, these plans can provide a regional framework that reduces automobile trips (and associated emissions), protects farmland from unnecessary development, conserves water and other essential natural resources, and achieves other sustainability goals. (See Figure 5.1.)

Figure 5.1. An illustration of the interrelation of plans across geographic scales

AECOM

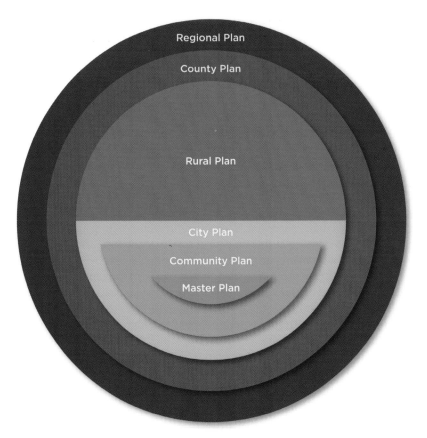

County, rural, and the various city and township comprehensive plans within a region can link jurisdictions that have land-use authority with the regional plan, promoting coordination at a regional level to help ensure that sustainable practices in one jurisdiction are not diminished by unsustainable practices in another. Only a few regional plans reviewed—notably those of the Twin Cities Metropolitan Council and the Tahoe Regional Planning Agency—have stronger implementation authority than local plans. These comprehensive plans establish the policies for sustaining places within a jurisdiction—where the transit-oriented and walkable districts will be located; how open space and habitat preserves will be connected; how water and energy can be best conserved; which economic infrastructure will be given priority; which policies will be employed to achieve balanced and healthy communities; and how the development of jobs and housing will be coordinated.

Community or subarea plans within a jurisdiction bring more precise definition to sustaining places by establishing land-use policies that provide the basis for zoning; articulate urban design parameters; identify historic resources; lay out infrastructure and public facility systems; and prioritize community development objectives that affect particular places and properties within the community—and do all this while remaining consistent with the county, city, or township plan.

Finally, the master plan adds structure and precision to the multiple components of a specific sustainable development subdivision, consistent with the community or city plan, such as land-use relationships and integration with surroundings; elements that support mobility infrastructure, connectivity, and complete streets; building design, site orientation, and relationships to the natural topography; water reclamation and distributive energy systems; parks, plazas, and open space and their interfaces with adjacent land uses; public facilities and services, including their financing; and other project elements.

The various levels of comprehensive plans within a region do not necessarily lead to sustainable outcomes. They could just as easily support unsustainable practices with different policies. If each plan is approached with the goal of sustaining places and the policies are mutually and internally consistent, however, the goal can be achieved over time. For an example of a vertically integrated plan supporting sustainable outcomes, see the case study of the San Diego Regional Planning Program in Appendix B.

Implementation can be the Achilles' heel of plans that are made to satisfy an intergovernmental mandate but that lack true local commitment. What can be built into a comprehensive plan for a sustainable community to ensure it actually gets carried out, rather than shelved and forgotten? The next chapter addresses the important role of implementation in sustaining the goals of the plan over time.

ENDNOTE

1. Funding for new HUD grants for Regional Plans for Sustainable Development was eliminated in H.R. 2112, the spending bill for fiscal year 2012. Limited funding was provided to implement and manage existing grants.

CHAPTER 6

Sustaining the Plan
Through Implementation

 Planning for implementation goes hand in hand with developing a plan. Support by decision makers and decisions on content, internal and external engagement, and financing set the stage for robust implementation. These decisions make the difference between a plan that has a long and active life and one that does not. Accountable implementation is the key principle behind long-lived and influential comprehensive plans.

Components of an effective implementation program include all of the following:

- Promotion of the plan after it has been adopted

- Local government adoption of an implementation strategy to assign responsibility and timelines for implementation; realigning the organization and budget process to achieve the plan; reviewing and updating codes and regulations to implement the plan's policies; revising environmental thresholds and discretionary review findings to be consistent with the new plan policies; identifying further work to be done; and establishing a process to measure progress and communicate the results

- Champions within the public, among elected officials, and within the bureaucracy to carry out the plan's implementation strategy and to continually monitor the plan's implementation results or shortcomings (e.g., some cities, such as Philadelphia, appoint a sustainability coordinator to champion sustainability policies and to follow up on progress in meeting goals)

- Commitment to implementation from all departments through establishment of a planning team with both backroom policy planners and frontline staff, as well as a system of reporting and mentoring by the higher-level government management team

- Adoption of policies and actions with time frames and implementation responsibilities assigned to departments or interdepartmental teams (e.g., responsibility for implementing Vancouver's transportation plan was assigned to a team comanaged by the directors of planning and engineering services)

- Coordination among the comprehensive plan, capital plan, and operating budgets to allocate funds for implementation and to hold responsible departments accountable

- Public commitment to plan implementation and to community participation in implementation actions to provide a bridge of memory in the community to remind elected officials and staff of implementation needs

- Adoption of sustainability metrics or indicators of success that are continuously monitored and regularly reported to the elected and appointed government officials and to the community interest groups and public at large (e.g., Seattle's Green Factor scores tabulate use of green roofs, permeable paving, tree preservation, and food cultivation)

- Recognition of involvement and celebration of milestones to refresh and maintain community support for implementation over time

While the comprehensive plan is the guiding policy document and action agenda for a city, county, or other governmental unit, the issues it addresses increasingly transcend the ability of any local jurisdiction to deal with them on its own (particularly in a time of increasing budget constraints). Thus, partnerships among the public, private, nonprofit, and institutional sectors (and across different levels of government) are becoming more and more important to effective implementation. A successful comprehensive planning process will involve representatives of these sectors (e.g., public schools, universities, health care institutions, local businesses, corporations, etc.) in developing the plan, with the goal of securing buy-in and, ultimately, commitments to participate in implementation.

THE ACTION ELEMENT

Comprehensive plans contain a mix of policy and action, and the tracking of action items is critical to successful plan implementation. To avoid a situation in which action items languish or are forgotten, an action element or plan is needed. A good action element will accomplish two objectives: (1) It will assign lead and supporting (or partner) agencies and a time frame to each action item so it is clear who is performing the action and when; and (2) it will provide a mechanism for tracking the implementation of actions. Lead and supporting agencies will typically be departments of planning, public works, and parks and recreation. Time frames for implementation are typically stated in terms of years from the date of plan adoption, such as short term (one to three years), medium term (three to five years), and long term (six or more years).

It is useful to gather all the action items from each chapter or element into a matrix. Maintaining this matrix as a spreadsheet will allow it to be sorted and searched by relevant fields, such as time frame, type, and lead agency. For example, a list of short- and medium-term actions involving capital projects would be of immediate use when developing a five-year capital improvement program. The City of Raleigh, North Carolina, has an action matrix in the implementation element of its comprehensive plan, which includes more than 500 discrete items. (About 120 of these items relate to development code amendments and are being considered as part of a major ordinance overhaul.) The City of Minneapolis employs a simpler and more manageable matrix of about 40 implementation strategies, with time frames, lead agencies, and partner agencies identified. The action matrix should be used to create to-do lists by time frame for each lead agency. It is the role of the planning department to track progress on these lists, but the directives to the other departments must come from the city or county manager or the governing body.

A report tracking the progress on action items or implementation strategies should be issued annually. Actions can be classified in one of four categories: completed; in progress; not started; or rejected. When an action item (e.g., a zoning amendment) is rejected or if actions languish past their deadline, guidance should be sought from the governing body as to whether the item is still warranted or should be removed with a plan amendment.

MONITORING THE PLAN

Tracking action items is only one simple element of plan monitoring. In the years after plan adoption, more fundamental questions regarding the plan will need to be answered, such as:

- Have staff and governmental officials been acting consistently with the policy guidance in the plan?

- Has any significant progress been made in achieving the overall goals and objectives of the plan? For example, if the plan sought to improve the quality and availability of public transit, have such changes led to ridership growth?

- Have there been any significant shifts in the data and trends that informed the original drafting of the plan? For example, has population growth been in line with projections? Has the economic base of the community changed in an unexpected way by the arrival or departure of a major industry? How has technological innovation changed outcomes? Have any new issues arisen in the communities that are not addressed in the plan? Are growth pressures or patterns of disinvestment emerging in areas previously thought to be stable? Have new environmental challenges appeared?

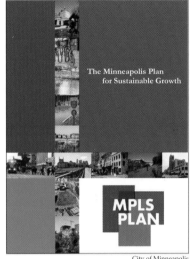

City of Minneapolis

Answering these questions requires appropriate monitoring mechanisms. Useful tools in this regard include:

• *Baseline data*: In order to monitor progress, it is necessary to establish baselines or starting points for each indicator, including the date when the baseline was established, its data source, and expected methods of updating it. When available, officially recognized public data sources, such as the U.S. Census and various state government indicators, can facilitate baseline setting.

• *Indicators:* Simple and easily obtainable metrics or data points are used to track overall progress on plan goals. Ideally, a set of indicators should be developed along with the plan. Plans with a focus on sustainability will need indicators that measure outcomes tied to the sustainability goals and objectives defined in the planning process. Such indicators might include, for example, transit ridership, vehicle-miles traveled, housing affordability, and agricultural lands preserved.

• *Data book*: Most comprehensive planning processes begin with a data inventory, trend analysis, and community audit. Periodically updating the data can verify whether the trends identified at the time the plan was crafted are still relevant. Given the work involved and the fact that trends do not reverse overnight, this should likely be done every three to five years, rather than annually.

• *Report cards/scorecards*: Cities such as Santa Monica and Minneapolis produce annual reports that document progress on sustainability indicators and implementation actions. These are in formats that are easy to read and compile so that members of the public can stay informed and engaged. For example, the Burlington Legacy Project issues an annual report card, scoring the implementation of each of its major components.

• *Policy tracking*: It should be standard operating procedure to note when any decision, such as a rezoning or ordinance text change, is approved that is inconsistent with plan policies. If certain policies have been repeatedly ignored or contradicted through decision or action, it will be necessary to revisit these policies with the governing body and the public.

A system of regular monitoring and updates is essential to maintain both the relevance and credibility of the plan. Plans that do not go through a regular reexamination and amendment process will be in danger of being dismissed as old and irrelevant. While most jurisdictions process minor amendments on an annual basis, a more thorough reexamination should be undertaken every five to 10 years and should include public input. This task will be easier if the data book and indicators have been kept up-to-date in the interim. Some communities will have an opportunity to partner with a local university to assist in devising indicators, collecting data, and analyzing results.

An example of sustainability indicators is found in the Marin Countywide Plan (Figure 6.1, page 61).

Finally, while plan monitoring and maintenance is important, it should not take precedence over other aspects of plan implementation. Planning departments vary greatly in terms of size and capability, and they should develop both their implementation plans and their monitoring programs while being mindful of their capacities.

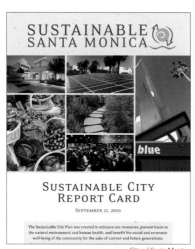

City of Santa Monica

PLANNING SUSTAINABLE COMMUNITIES

How Success Is Measured

INDICATOR	BENCHMARK	TARGET
Number of dwelling units within ½ mile of a transit stop	82,773 dwelling units	89,997 dwelling units
Energy use per capita countywide	16,636 kWh unincorporated per capita in 2000	Reduce consumption of electricity per capita 10% by 2020
Total megawatts of photovoltaic systems installed countywide	0.0255 MW in 2000	15 MW by 2015 and 30 MW by 2020
Total megawatts of photovoltaic systems installed by County government	0 MW in 2000	0.5 MW by 2010 and 1 MW by 2015
Regional fair share housing allocation	Met in 2000	Meet regional fair share allocation in 2010 and 2015
Jobs-housing balance countywide	1.22 workers per household in 2000	Reach and maintain a 1.3-employed-resident-workers-to total-jobs ratio through 2015
Number of employees who live and work in Marin	61% in 2000	No decrease
Number of vehicles with a fuel economy of at least 45 miles per gallon countywide	362 in 2002	Increase the number of zero and partial zero emission vehicles with a fuel economy of at least 45 mpg through 2020
Vehicle miles traveled overall countywide (VMT)	2,764 million VMT in 2000	No or minimal increase through 2015
Miles of class I and II bicycle pathways in unincorporated areas	3.5 miles of class I in 2000 and 2.25 miles of class II in 2000	Increase to 4.5–10 miles by 2010 and 9–25 miles by 2015
Public transportation ridership share of modal split countywide	11% (bus and ferry) in 2000	Increase public transportation ridership by 2015, again by 2020
Per capita use of potable water	299 gallons daily per capita in 2000	No increase through 2020
Per capita use of non-potable water for appropriate end use	5 gallons daily per capita in 2000	Increase through 2020
Percent of solid waste diverted from landfills	Diversion rate was 65% in 2000	Increase diversion rate to 75% by 2010 and 80% by 2015

Figure 6.1. Sustainability indicators from the Marin Countywide Plan

County of Marin

UPDATING THE PLAN

Comprehensive plans must be updated on a regular basis in order to stay abreast of changing conditions and needs. The usual practice, required by states such as Florida, is to conduct a formal plan evaluation and update every five to eight years. General plans in California are comprehensively updated approximately every 20 years, with housing elements updated every five to eight years. Many updates are more or less routine; new information and projections are incorporated, but basic policies and plan elements undergo only incremental change. When a jurisdiction decides to undertake sustainable planning, however, the changes are more fundamental. Some pioneering communities opt to completely rewrite their plans in order to create a totally new model; most others make the switch on a more gradual basis.

Raleigh, North Carolina, recently updated its plan through inclusion of a number of sustaining places features, but it did not completely abandon the traditional format. Its experience is illuminating for those communities that are making a more gradual transition to a sustainable plan. (See sidebar.)

INCORPORATING SUSTAINABILITY INTO THE CITY OF RALEIGH, NORTH CAROLINA, COMPREHENSIVE PLAN UPDATE

When Raleigh set out to overhaul its comprehensive plan in 2007, the adopted plan was less than 20 years old but was increasingly seen as out of step with the times. In particular, the 1989 plan did not incorporate current thinking on sustainability. Certain components of the plan, however, were supported by engaged and vocal constituencies—meaning that the new plan had to identify and preserve what was best about the old one. As a result, the process of creating the new plan combined an emphasis on fresh visioning and thinking with a careful audit of adopted policy guidance.

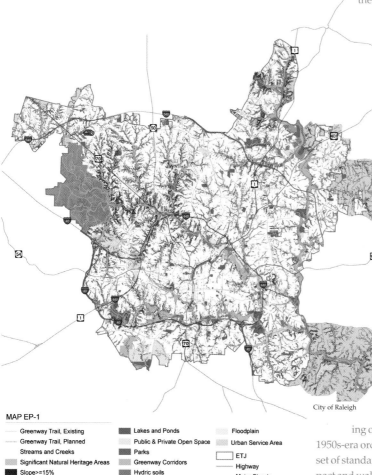

MAP EP-1

- Greenway Trail, Existing
- Greenway Trail, Planned
- Streams and Creeks
- Significant Natural Heritage Areas
- Slope>=15%
- Lakes and Ponds
- Public & Private Open Space
- Parks
- Greenway Corridors
- Hydric soils
- Floodplain
- Urban Service Area
- ETJ
- Highway
- Major Streets

City of Raleigh

the word "sustainable" appears in only one of the theme titles, all three legs of the sustainability stool—economy, equity, and environment—are accounted for.

The public outreach process was accompanied by an equally intensive "inreach" effort aimed at the many city departments ultimately bearing responsibility for plan implementation. Two key goals of this process were to break down the silos that had produced the uncoordinated "system" elements in the 1989 plan and to instill a sense of ownership of the document throughout the city's administration. In the end, nearly every department played an active role in some aspect of plan drafting, review, and adoption.

Raleigh's adopted 2030 Comprehensive Plan represents an important but interim step toward a more sustainable future. The plan retains a traditional structure consisting of topical elements, such as land use, transportation, and housing, but the plan also incorporates many features that are new for Raleigh, including its first-ever citywide land-use plan to guide growth; an environmental protection element with a specific section addressing climate change adaptation and mitigation; strong links between land use and transportation; an implementation element that includes mechanisms for tracking action items and keeping the plan current; and the theme of sustainability threaded through each and every plan element.

Eighteen months after adoption, the 2030 Comprehensive Plan is widely recognized as providing thoughtful and practical guidance for the future development of the city. Implementation is off to a strong start, marred only by one instance where an environmental goal ran afoul of entrenched property interests. Raleigh is now well into a sweeping overhaul of its development code, which will replace a 1950s-era ordinance with a modern, more urban, and form-centric set of standards that will do away with regulatory barriers to compact and walkable development. Such an undertaking would have been unthinkable without the new policy framework provided by the new plan. When adopted, the new code will implement 120 of the approximately 550 action items in the plan.

One key lesson from Raleigh's experience is that, while a focus on sustainability was an easy sell to the community (it sounds progressive and appears to ask little of the public, at least in the short term), getting city department heads on board was the greater challenge because they would be the first to incur the cost and disruption caused by new ways of conducting business. The internal culture change that the process of plan development and implementation has helped to foster has been one of the most valuable outcomes of Raleigh's comprehensive sustainable planning effort.

audit revealed a plan bloated with nearly 5,000 policy statements and action items, many of which had never been implemented, while the inventory painted the portrait of a successful community waking to the consequences of 70 years of sprawling postwar growth.

Using these findings as a launching point, the first round of public workshops produced six vision themes that formed the overarching goals for the plan: (1) Economic prosperity and equity; (2) expanding housing choices; (3) managing our growth; (4) coordinating land use and transportation; (5) Greenprint Raleigh—sustainable development; and (6) growing successful neighborhoods and communities. Every policy later developed for the plan had to link back to one or more of these themes. While

ADAPTING THE PLAN

A successful comprehensive plan is used and updated on an ongoing basis. An effective monitoring program, including periodic checkups and tracking of indicators to measure implementation progress, is essential. Given the long-range time horizon of the comprehensive plan and the difficulty of projecting the future in an era of uncertainty and constant change, implementation must be flexible enough to allow decision makers to adapt to new and unforeseen circumstances. For example, how many comprehensive plans prepared in 2005 anticipated the collapse of the housing market and the Great Recession a few years later? Looking toward the future, how can we properly plan for the impacts of climate change given the range of possibilities (sea-level rise, precipitation changes, etc.) predicted by scientists? When will the "peak oil" phenomenon predicted by many experts actually occur—or has it occurred already, only masked by the recession? When will gas price escalation profoundly shift people's transportation and housing location choices?

This inherent uncertainty is epitomized by the need to design local policies in the comprehensive plan to adapt to climate change based on scientific models that characterize future impacts in terms of probabilities and ranges. The unknown level of commitment that the global community will make to mitigate GHG emissions puts more responsibilities on localities. A further complicating factor is the skepticism of a significant segment of the public regarding the reality of climate change. To address these uncertainties, climate change adaptation strategies need to be flexible and implemented incrementally over time, thus making costs more manageable and avoiding waste (e.g., expensive engineering solutions built for the wrong scenario). One emerging approach, termed anticipatory governance, is to use scenarios and continuous monitoring of indicators and evidence in order to update plans and policies in real time (Quay 2010).

Most commonly used by natural resource managers, adaptive management is an interactive process of improving management practices and decision making by learning from the outcomes of previous practices and decisions. Applied to a policy instrument like the comprehensive plan, this basic concept can be used to periodically recalibrate an implementation program by assessing the results of past actions and aligning future actions with new knowledge of the trends that will shape a community's future. In the case of climate change adaptation, this would mean (science permitting) identifying and monitoring climate factors most closely tied to local impacts to allow sufficient time to respond through action (Quay 2010, 507). In another example, data indicators related to economic, environmental, or social factors (e.g., growth rate, vehicle-miles traveled, public health outcomes, educational attainment) could be periodically measured against goals and projections used in developing future scenarios during the planning process. The results would be used to adapt plan implementation based on improved understanding of the outcomes of past actions and the context for future actions.

Sustaining the plan through community implementation is one critical key to the long-range effectiveness of the sustaining places planning process. Another key is national support from the professional planning and public interest associations that advocate sustaining places policies and programs, as discussed in Chapter 7.

Conclusions and Recommendations: An Agenda for Sustaining Places

 We are at a critical turning point in the practice of comprehensive planning. Now is the time when the comprehensive plan can and should be the foremost tool in our responses to the critical sustainability challenges facing communities, nations, and the planet itself. Now is the time when effective plans can spearhead the revolution necessary to realize sustainable urban development. Now is the time when the creative ideas and energy of planners can be joined with those of professionals in related fields to develop new methods and ways of responding to the challenges posed by climate change, energy shortages, and natural disasters. In short, now is the time for the planning profession to shape and implement a bold new agenda for sustaining places.

As we have demonstrated, the most important tool for sustaining places is the comprehensive plan, a document with legal standing backed by a history of applications at all scales of settlement. Such plans must be prepared with attention to the concept of planning for sustaining places, defined by the APA Task Force on Sustaining Places as:

> a dynamic, democratic process through which communities plan to meet the needs of current and future generations without compromising the ecosystems upon which they depend by balancing social, economic, and environmental resources, incorporating resilience, and linking local actions to regional and global concerns.

This chapter lays out an agenda for those who make and implement comprehensive plans for sustaining places. It identifies goals for revising and updating existing plans in order to foster sustainable outcomes. It provides a framework of principles for preparing new plans aimed at sustaining towns, cities, and regions. It calls on the American Planning Association (APA) and the American Institute of Certified Planners (AICP) to support this agenda through an active program of professional development and plan certification.

MAKING AND IMPLEMENTING COMPREHENSIVE PLANS FOR SUSTAINING PLACES

Communities seeking to sustain themselves through comprehensive planning need to consider how to organize their resources to do so. The first step is to make a commitment to sustainability, in which the community and its leaders declare themselves committed to linking their actions with sustainability goals and measures. This must be allied with a public engagement process that enlists citizens in an intensive effort to envision a community as a sustainable and sustaining place. The outcome of these actions should be the preparation of a comprehensive plan that implements the vision of sustainability through a coordinated set of policies, priorities, and public expenditures.

A number of leading contemporary plans are taking up the challenge of planning for sustaining places. A set of best practices emerges from these plans. Based on the APA Task Force's review of these practices (Chapter 1), the resulting comprehensive plan should:

- *Adopt sustainability principles* to guide planning and decision making and to commit the community to sustainability as a high priority.

- *Coordinate and integrate policies and actions* from separate functional plans—such as climate change, hazard mitigation, community health, housing, environmental quality, food security, and others—into the overall framework of the comprehensive plan.

- *Influence development decisions* to improve and to sustain people's livelihoods, their living and working places, and their environmental resources by ensuring fair distribution of benefits and burdens and equitable access to public facilities.

- *Act on scientific evidence* regarding anticipated changes in global economic and environmental systems and their local consequences through mitigation and adaptation.

- *Recognize the need to address multiple sustainability demands with limited funds* in times of fiscal stress.

- *Implement sustainability goals* that seek to cope with an increasingly uncertain future, much of it unfolding on a continuous basis and determined globally rather than locally.

- *Identify and monitor sustainability metrics* to measure progress toward reaching plan goals and objectives and to inform decision makers and the community about the status of sustainability issues.

- *Make explicit linkages to regional plans and actions* to incorporate environmental and economic processes operating beyond the local scale.

- *Promote collaborative multistakeholder processes* that engage the full range of community interests and leaders so as to ensure public involvement and education about sustainability issues and needs.

Whether the goal is to revise an existing plan or to prepare a new plan, certain principles should guide both the planning process and the plan content. These principles do not determine the specific planning techniques to be used; instead, they are guideposts for framing and evaluating the plan. As derived from the APA Task Force's review of leading comprehensive plans (Chapter 2), these principles include:

- *Livable Built Environment*—ensure that all elements of the built environment, including land use, transportation, housing, energy, and infrastructure, work together to provide sustainable, green places for living, working, and recreation, with a high quality of life.

- *Harmony with Nature*—ensure that the contributions of natural resources to human well-being are explicitly recognized and valued and that maintaining their health is a primary objective.

- *Resilient Economy*—ensure that the community is prepared to deal with both positive and negative changes in its economic health and to initiate sustainable urban development and redevelopment strategies that foster green business growth and build reliance on local assets.

- *Interwoven Equity*—ensure fairness and equity in providing for the housing, services, health, safety, and livelihood needs of all citizens and groups.

- *Healthy Community*—ensure that public health needs are recognized and addressed through provisions for healthy foods, physical activity, access to recreation, health care, environmental justice, and safe neighborhoods.

- *Responsible Regionalism*—ensure that all local proposals account for, connect with, and support the plans of adjacent jurisdictions and the surrounding region.

- *Authentic Participation*—ensure that the planning process actively involves all segments of the community in analyzing issues, generating visions, developing plans, and monitoring outcomes.

- *Accountable Implementation*—ensure that responsibilities for carrying out the plan are clearly stated, along with metrics for evaluating progress in achieving desired outcomes.

One way to encourage the spread of sustaining places planning is to create a plan certification program. Plans developed according to these principles should be able to be certified as sustaining places comprehensive plans if they also share the following characteristics:

1. **Formal Governmental Support.** The plan must contain evidence that its governing body formally supports the goals and principles of sustaining places, provides funding and budgetary resources to achieve the plan's goals and objectives, and directs its officials and staff to implement the policies contained in the plan. The plan should demonstrate the government's intent to carry forward its actions through subsequent priorities, programs, and annual budgets.

2. **Sustaining Places Principles.** The plan must be built around the principles for planning for sustaining places and contain specific language, analysis, goals, objectives, policies, and maps to achieve these principles in practice.

3. **Integrated Comprehensive Plan.** The plan must be designed to integrate proposals for land use, mobility, housing, economic development, environmental quality, public facilities, and other areas so as to address critical issues of climate change, energy, food supply, and related topics sometimes addressed in separate plans.

4. **Regional Coordination and Consistency.** The plan must be coordinated and consistent with other related plans in the region.

5. **Implementation Metrics.** The plan must identify responsibilities for implementation and contain provisions for monitoring and reporting on achievement with metrics that document success or failure to meet its goals, objectives, and priorities.

Planning for sustaining places is a joint effort of citizens, elected officials, and government staff, all involved in coproducing a comprehensive plan tailored to the needs of their community. City and regional planners play leading roles in these processes, helping to structure citizen participation efforts, providing data and analyses of community problems and needs, and assisting in writing and implementing the formal plan documents. Planners should draw on their professional organizations for supporting research and training.

Planning organizations can contribute to the effectiveness of planning for sustaining places through several means. They can establish a professional culture that recognizes and fosters the growth of applications in planning practice and education for sustaining places. They can conduct research and development aimed at building a repertoire of knowledge, concepts, and techniques pertinent to sustaining places. They can explore the potential of a sustaining places certification program for comprehensive plans. And they can develop education and awareness activities aimed at widening public and professional understanding of the potential and importance of planning for sustaining places.

As a prominent organization with nationwide membership, the American Planning Association (APA) and its professional institute, the American Institute of Certified Planners (AICP), can continue to engender a culture of practice and education about effective ways to sustain places through their policies and programs. Planners and others concerned with sustaining places can turn to APA and AICP for professional programs, publications, public recognition of best practices, research projects, and educational outreach in this developing field.

CALL TO ACTION

We conclude that the planning profession faces an unprecedented opportunity to make a critical difference in the places where people live now and in the future. We risk losing the trust of our fellow professionals and our constituencies if we fail to seize this opportunity and claim the leadership role in furthering public interest in sustaining places. The need is clear, the agenda is on point, and the resources are at hand. It is time for us to accept the challenge.

Plan Analyses

To identify and to understand the practice of planning for sustainable places, the task force analyzed selected plans of each type, describing their approaches, characteristics, and innovations. We based our selection on reputation, adoption status, and the need to include plans at various scales, geographic locations, and for growing versus stable or declining populations. Our selection is not intended to imply a ranking but simply represents pragmatic choices among a broad group of promising and best practices. We recognize that leading-edge plans are in process but not yet adopted. Given the emerging state of practice, we expect that the number and quality of plans for sustaining places will continue to grow at a rapid rate.

These plans were analyzed in this report:

- the 2005 Toward a Sustainable Seattle Plan (www.seattle.gov/dpd/Planning/Seattle_s_Comprehensive_Plan/Overview)

- the 2007 Marin Countywide Plan (www.co.marin.ca.us)

- the 2011 Plan Fort Collins (www.fcgov.com/advanceplanning/city-plan.php)

- the Regional Comprehensive Plan for the San Diego Region (www.sandag.org)

- the Keene, New Hampshire, 2010 Comprehensive Master Plan (www.ci.keene.nh.us/departments/planning/keene-cmp-2010)

- the Burlington, Vermont, 2000 Legacy Plan (http://burlingtonlegacyproject.org/files/2009/07/LegacyActionPlan.pdf)

- the 2009 Union County, Pennsylvania, Cultivating Community Comprehensive Plan (www.cultivatingcommunity.net/draft-plan,html)

- the Philadelphia 2035 Plan (http://phila2035.org)

- the Albany, New York, 2030 Comprehensive Plan (http://albany2030.org)

- the Connecting Cleveland 2020 Citywide Plan (http://planning.city.cleveland.oh.us/cwp/cpc.html).

For each of the plans, we have included a brief narrative description of its features and unique attributes, as well as a table that evaluates the extent to which each plan incorporates and addresses the principles of planning for sustaining places set forth in Chapter 2 of this report. To complete the assessments, each plan was read and analyzed by two members of the task force, using an approach similar to one described in Norton 2008. We recognize that it is possible to carry out more rigorous, extensive, and academic plan comparisons and evaluations (e.g., see http://sustainabilityplanninglab.wordpress.com and Berke and Godschalk 2009), but we found this approach to be useful in highlighting the state of practice of planning for sustaining places.

TOWARD A SUSTAINABLE SEATTLE

One of the earliest plans for sustaining a place was adopted by Seattle in 1994. The story of its evolution describes the arc that such plans have followed and illustrates the emerging practice of sustainability planning.

The Seattle Comprehensive Plan defines a sustainable city in the following terms:

> Sustainable cities use resources efficiently and effectively. They reuse and they recycle. They recognize constraints and build on assets. They use existing local resources where they can. They minimize exportation of environmental risk. They provide physical and economic security, and they distribute these and other benefits evenly. They balance the need for growth with the needs of stability and prudent use of resources. (viii)

The plan identifies four core values that together "become a foundation upon which to build a sustainable future for ourselves and the generations to follow":

- Community

- Environmental stewardship

- Economic opportunity and security

- Social equity

The centerpiece of the current plan (2005) remains what it was in 1994, an Urban Villages Strategy: identifying, strengthening, and densifying mixed use activity centers in the city and accommodating a significant share of regional population and employment growth. The plan lays out a typology of these urban villages, giving much of the responsibility for determining what they would look like and how density is to be accommodated to the neighborhoods themselves and a strong neighborhood-planning process. The types are Urban Centers, Manufacturing/Industrial Centers, Hub Urban Villages, and Residential Urban Villages, each envisioning different characters, uses, and density levels (with density and job growth targets now set to 2024).

Empowering neighborhoods has been a key feature of Seattle planning, providing them with planning budgets and help from the city's office of neighborhood planning. The plan, and its vision and targets for urban villages, stipulates the minimum criteria neighborhoods must respect in preparing their plans.

The Seattle plan includes strong environmental and energy elements, embracing the precautionary principle and advancing a series of strong goals and policies. Specific topics include natural drainage and urban watershed protection, tree protection and urban forest management (setting a goal of a 1 percent increase per year in tree canopy coverage until reaching 40 percent), and climate change. All new city buildings are to be designed to be carbon neutral by 2030.

Seattle's plan is comprehensive in scope, including (among others) economic development, human development, and cultural resources elements. The plan clearly recognizes the need to consider economic, social, and cultural values, as well as environmental ones, in reaching a sustainable future.

The plan addresses a wide range of sustainability issues, from energy to water to urban green spaces, often in innovative ways. Water reduction and energy provisions have worked especially well, as shown by the city's achievement of a one-quarter reduction in energy consumption through the plan's conservation measures.

The plan has not been perfect, and many of the social goals have not yet been attained. Seattle neighborhoods with a high degree of poverty when the plan was unveiled in 1994 remain impoverished today. While the plan has been updated several times, it has been seven years since the last update, and the city is just beginning that process with the hope that a new version will be in place in 2012.

In addition to its groundbreaking comprehensive plan, Seattle has a broad range of innovative planning and sustainability initiatives that continue to inspire. Seattle has pioneered and piloted low-impact development and innovative stormwater management techniques, for instance, and has also been a leader in green building. Seattle's unique Green Factor requirement stipulates that new commercial development and multifamily housing in certain designated zones must meet a minimum standard on a green-feature scoring system. Projects achieve points by including features such as green rooftops, vegetated walls, tree canopy coverage, and permeable paving. Bonus points are available for use of drought-tolerant and native plants and for "landscaping in food cultivation."

Seattle's pioneering plan for a sustainable city combines principles of smart growth, urban design, and public participation with principles for creating a sustainable place. In practice, these principles reinforce one another as part of a comprehensive planning package that balances environmental, equity, and economic values—a goal derived from the earliest definition of sustainable development.

TOWARD A SUSTAINABLE SEATTLE

Seattle's pioneering plan for a sustainable city combines principles of smart growth, urban design, and public participation with principles of a sustainable place. In practice, these principles reinforce one another as part of a comprehensive planning package that balances environmental, equity, and economic values—a goal derived from the earliest definition of sustainable development.

TOWARD A SUSTAINABLE SEATTLE SCORECARD

	Low	Moderate	High
Livable Built Environment. The plan focuses on urban villages, transit-oriented development (TOD), and multimodal transportation; it emphasizes an integrated approach to planning, environment, and design.			X
Harmony with Nature. The plan has strong environmental and energy elements, including watershed protection, tree protection, and urban forest management.			X
Resilient Economy. The economy is not one of the emphases of the plan.		X	
Interwoven Equity. The plan emphasizes empowering neighborhoods.			X
Healthy Community. The plan is very good on this criterion.			X
Responsible Regionalism. The plan could be improved.		X	
Authentic Participation. The plan provides for extensive outreach and has an educational component.			X
Accountable Implementation. The plan sets ambitious and innovative goals for the urban villages strategy, but the implementation procedures were not specific.		X	

MARIN, CALIFORNIA, COUNTYWIDE PLAN

The Marin Countywide Plan, adopted in 2007, is a lengthy (more than 650-page) document whose framework is defined as planning sustainable communities. It is an educational plan in that it begins with an explanation of sustainability within the context of the county and provides background information on each of the goals it lays out.

Plan goals are evaluated for their environmental, economic, and social equity benefits, and the plan answers the following questions in order for readers to better understand each of the goals and policies:

- What are the desired outcomes?

- Why is the goal or policy important (with a focus on addressing the three Es)?

- How will the results be achieved?

- How will success be measured?

The three main sections of the plan are the Natural Systems and Agriculture Element (nature and life-support systems); the Built Environment Element (villages, towns, and construction-related activities); and the Socioeconomic Element (people and what they do for each other).

The plan measures and tracks success with benchmarks and targets for various indicators. A website measures baseline data against targets, using criteria and public performance indicators that are easy to track (http://marin.visiblestrategies.com). The goals of the plan are directly related to sustainability:

1. Link equity, economy, and the environment locally, regionally, and globally.

2. Minimize the use of finite resources and use all resources efficiently and effectively.

3. Reduce the use and minimize the release of hazardous materials.

4. Reduce greenhouse gas emissions that contribute to global warming.

5. Preserve our natural assets.

6. Protect our agricultural assets.

7. Provide efficient and effective transportation.

MARIN COUNTYWIDE PLAN

Each element of the Marin Countywide Plan asks the following questions:

- What are the desired outcomes?

- Why is this important?

- How will results be achieved?

- How will success be measured?

The answers to these questions are organized into respective goals, policies, implementation programs, and a series of indicators, benchmarks, and targets for each topic area in the plan.

8. Supply housing affordable to the full range of our members of the workforce and diverse community.

9. Foster businesses that create economic, environmental, and social benefits.

10. Educate and prepare our workforce and residents.

11. Cultivate ethnic, cultural, and socioeconomic diversity.

12. Support public health, safety, and social justice.

The principles of the Marin Countywide Plan are supportive of the fundamental sustainability principles.

MARIN COUNTYWIDE PLAN SCORECARD

	Low	Moderate	High
Livable Built Environment. The plan integrates community design, green building, housing, transportation, and infrastructure.			X
Harmony with Nature. The plan addresses biological and water resources, environmental hazards, atmosphere and climate, and open space.			X
Resilient Economy. The plan focuses on attracting and retaining businesses, green businesses, and targeted industries.			X
Interwoven Equity. Equity is the number-one goal of the plan.			X
Healthy Community. The plan emphasizes access to healthy food, local agriculture, and community health.			X
Responsible Regionalism. The plan focuses on Marin County.		X	
Authentic Participation. The plan is structured for maximum citizen understanding and involvement.			X
Accountable Implementation. The plan has a strong emphasis on measuring and monitoring results and has specific actions for implementation.			X

SUSTAINABILITY IN FORT COLLINS PLAN

The basic tenets of sustainability serve as guiding principles for the plan's vision and underpin all components:

- A focus on the future with a long-term perspective (an outlook for the generations to come)

- An understanding that the community is bounded by the limits of the natural world and its resources

- A systems perspective that recognizes the interdependent economic, human, and environmental implications of policies, decisions, and outcomes

- A mechanism for continuous improvement through monitoring and future plan updates ◄

FORT COLLINS, COLORADO, 2011 CITY PLAN

In early 2011, the City of Fort Collins, Colorado, adopted a new comprehensive plan as part of its Plan Fort Collins process, an integrated process to prepare major updates to two key documents: the city plan and the transportation master plan. The new plan structure is fundamentally based on the city's Budgeting for Outcomes process in order to align the city's planning and policy directions with its budgeting process. Its organization is designed to be simple and easily understood by a variety of audiences and is structured in seven chapters:

- Economic health

- Environmental health

- Community and neighborhood livability

- Safety and wellness

- Culture, parks, and recreation

- High-performing community

- Transportation

The bulk of each chapter is allocated to principles and policies. Principles provide general rules or directions for the city or community to follow, whereas policies specify more definite courses to follow for future decisions or actions.

Sustainability in the Plan

In addition to being a core component of the community vision and planning process, the topic of sustainability is integrated throughout the plan documents. Each chapter of the city plan features a section on the following items:

- The topic's relationship to the economic, environmental, and human aspects of sustainability

- A list of possible indicators to measure progress related to the topic

- A summary table (see table) that details how the topic closely connects and relates to principles and policies in other chapters

	Economic Health	Community and Neighborhood Livability	Safety and Wellness	Culture, Parks, and Recreation	High Performing Community	Transportation
Conservation & Stewardship		• Tree preservation and ecologically sound landscape design (LIV 10, 14)		• Environmental best management practices in parks and recreation areas (CPR 4)	• Collaboration with private citizens and organizations (HI 3, 4)	
Open Lands		• Connected system of open lands (Structure Map theme, LIV 23, 40, 41, 42, 45, 46) • Clustered residential development (LIV 27)	• Opportunities for recreation and active lifestyles (SW 2) • Food production (SW 3)	• Interconnected system of open lands (CPR 4) • Multi-purpose lands (CPR 5)	• Engagement and learning (HI 2, 3) • Forge partnerships and collaborate regionally (HI 4)	• Interface with open lands (T 4) • Connected system of trails (T 11)
Energy	• Innovation in clean energy industry cluster (EH 2)	• Energy conservation and efficiency in housing (LIV 9)	• Emergency management and the electric grid (SW 1)		• Engagement and learning (HI 2, 3) • Technological solutions (HI 6, 7)	• New vehicle types (T 17) • Transportation energy use impacts (T 30)
Air Quality		• Multiple means of travel to reduce vehicle miles traveled (Structure Map theme, LIV 21, 30, 35, 36, 37, 43, 44, 45)	• Enforcement of health ordinances (SW 2)		• Engagement and learning (HI 2, 3) • Forge partnerships and collaborate regionally (HI 4)	• Transportation Demand Management to reduce vehicle miles traveled and improve air quality (T 3, 27, 30)
Climate		• Reduced carbon emissions (Structure Map theme)	• Emergency preparedness and weather events (SW 1)		• Engagement and learning (HI 2, 3) • Forge partnerships and collaborate regionally (HI 4)	• Transportation Demand Management to reduce greenhouse gas emissions (T 27, 30)
Waste		• Adaptive reuse of historic structures (LIV 16, 17)	• Emergency management and hazardous materials (SW 1)		• Engagement and learning (HI 2, 3) • Forge partnerships and collaborate regionally (HI 4)	
Stormwater	• Encourage redevelopment by reducing stormwater infrastructure barriers (EH 4)	• Adequate public facilities with development (LIV 4)	• Emergency management and flooding (SW 1)	• Multi-purpose lands (CPR 5)	• Engagement and learning (HI 2, 3) • Forge partnerships and collaborate regionally (HI 4)	• Green streets (T 24)
Water Resources	• Innovation in water industry cluster (EH 2)	• Adequate public facilities with development (LIV 4) • Water efficiency and conservation (LIV 9, 14)		• Untreated water for irrigation in appropriate areas (CPR 4)	• Engagement and learning (HI 2, 3) • Forge partnerships and collaborate regionally (HI 4)	

There are many examples of how sustainability is addressed as a topic, but, more important, sustainability was a key driver from the beginning of the Plan Fort Collins effort. Specifically, three main tenets of sustainability—systems thinking, continuous improvement, and triple-bottom-line analysis—were integrated into the process and emphasized within each of the chapters of the city plan.

Systems thinking. Plan Fort Collins recognizes that principles, policies, strategies, and actions should not be developed and implemented in isolation from one another or work at cross-purposes. Throughout the update process, the planning team used and encouraged systems thinking to recognize and emphasize the interrelationships among the plan components. As a result, the plan highlights the interrelationships among topics throughout the plans, from broad topic areas to specific principles and key policy choices. In this context, sustainability functioned as a unifying concept—a way to integrate and connect topics across city service areas and departments, as well as throughout the community, to explore options to address current and future needs efficiently and effectively.

Continuous improvement. In order to be effective, planning must be not static but rather always dynamic, incorporating a process of planning, taking action, checking progress, and acting to change course where needed. While Fort Collins generally has a continuous improvement model already in place, their new plan establishes a more effective framework for decision making and continuous improvement by creating stronger links among monitoring tools and indicators, ongoing plan refinements and policy adjustments, and implementation.

Triple-bottom-line analysis. To integrate the concept of sustainability across all phases of the planning process, a triple-bottom-line perspective was used during the planning process to support and inform decision making. Triple-bottom-line analysis, which has been used by leading-edge communities and organizations around the world, incorporates environmental, economic, and human considerations so that principles, policies, strategies, and implementing actions are developed with consideration of the benefits and trade-offs across all three of these topic areas.

FORT COLLINS CITY PLAN SCORECARD

	Low	Moderate	High
Livable Built Environment. The plan's Community and Neighborhood Livability section addresses this principle in detail.			X
Harmony with Nature. The plan addresses air quality, land and resource conservation, energy, climate, waste, water resources, and stormwater.			X
Resilient Economy. The plan focuses on targeted industry clusters in the innovation economy, local businesses ("Uniquely Fort Collins"), and partnerships with education and industry.			X
Interwoven Equity. Equity is addressed in various sections—High-Performing Community, Transportation, Healthy Community—but not as extensively as in other plans reviewed.		X	
Healthy Community. The plan includes an element that addresses community health, safety, and local food access and production.			X
Responsible Regionalism. Regional cooperation is a strong theme in topics related to land use, transportation, environment, and economy.			X
Authentic Participation. The High-Performing Community section ocuses on engaging the community in the planning process as well as in community building and collaborative problem solving.			X
Accountable Implementation. The plan has a strong emphasis on measuring and monitoring results, and has specific actions to implement the plan.			X

SAN DIEGO COUNTY—THE 2004 REGIONAL COMPREHENSIVE PLAN (RCP) FOR THE SAN DIEGO REGION

One of the largest and most ambitious regional planning efforts in the United States, the San Diego region is a model of the vertical integration of sustainable plans—coordinating the comprehensive plans of the county and its 19 municipalities as well as their transportation and open space plans. (See Appendix B.) Like most regional planning agencies, the San Diego Association of Governments (SANDAG) does not exercise land-use authority. However, unlike many regional planning agencies, the San Diego Regional Comprehensive Plan (RCP) has implementation powers through its control of funding for regional transportation infrastructure and habitat acquisition, as well as its role in applying state environmental laws that set GHG emission-reduction targets. The region's sustainable planning system, as set forth in the RCP, is built on a combination of financing incentives, regulations, and consensus building, in addition to the individual general plans of the member agencies that are prepared independently but coordinated with the RCP.

The San Diego region is coterminous with the 4,200 square miles of San Diego County, where regional planning is carried out by SANDAG. SANDAG's regional comprehensive planning started in the 1980s as a growth management initiative to respond to concerns about growth impacts and traffic congestion. SANDAG obtained voter approval for a half-cent sales tax for transportation (known as TransNet), which has provided $3.3 billion in transportation funding over a 20-year period, leveraging state and federal transportation dollars. SANDAG also was designated by a countywide voter initiative as a "regional growth management" organization with responsibilities to monitor growth impacts on public facilities and the environment. At the same time, local jurisdictions agreed to habitat conservation plans (HCPs) that designated 472,000 acres of the region as protected habitats for 85 animal and plant species in exchange for allowing development in nondesignated areas. In 2003, the California legislature gave SANDAG the authority to adopt an RCP that would use regional transportation funds for implementation and would monitor progress through measurable standards and criteria.

Preparation of the current RCP was spearheaded by the SANDAG Regional Planning Committee, made up of local elected officials representing six county subregions, advisory members representing federal, state, and regional public agencies, and a representative of the Technical Working Group (comprising the planning directors of the member agencies). Adopted in 2004, the RCP was designed to build on the regional transportation plan while addressing environmental issues in the context of a comprehensive plan. The regional plan was organized along the lines of local general plans, with transportation, land-use and urban form, housing, economic development, environment, and public facilities elements, and also addressed interregional and binational issues (in recognition of the adjacent Tijuana-Rosario-Ensenada metro area in Mexico). It included a five-year action plan and a performance-monitoring program.

Plan implementation proceeded through two strategic initiatives. First, a ballot initiative extending the existing TransNet half-cent sales tax was approved by voters. This tax measure, which was focused primarily on providing funding for transportation system improvements and operating programs, also included a budget of $850 million for the Environmental Mitigation Program to enable acquisition of habitat mitigation land for new transportation projects, as well as $280 million for the Smart Growth Incentive Program to provide grants to local governments for smart growth planning and community infrastructure. Second, in 2006 SANDAG accepted a "Smart Growth Concept Map" prepared by staff and local planning directors to identify smart growth opportunity areas and open space preserve areas contained in the region's adopted HCPs. This map is used to prioritize transportation investments and allocate regional funding for local infrastructure improvements in the TransNet Smart Growth Incentive Program.

Recent implementation is guided by two California laws: the 2006 Global Warming Solutions Act (AB32) and the 2008 Steinberg Act (SB375). AB32 sets statewide GHG reduction targets, while SB375 establishes a procedure for identifying and implementing regional GHG reduction targets; it requires metropolitan planning organizations (MPOs) such as SANDAG to meet these targets through updates of their Regional Transportation Plans (RTP) and their Regional Housing Needs Assessment (RHNA) Plans including potential affordable housing. It requires regions with MPOs to adopt Sustainable Communities Strategies as part of their

SAN DIEGO REGIONAL PLAN

SANDAG's regional plan integrates comprehensive, transportation, and open space plans at the regional scale, coordinated with city, community, and project scales. In response to California laws, the region's plans aim to meet GHG-reduction goals through coordinated funding of transportation, open space, and smart growth initiatives. The planning system is implemented through financial incentives, regulations, and consensus building.

regional transportation plans. SANDAG's draft RTP attains the required targets through a number of measures, including land-use strategies to enhance compact development near public transit, transportation system improvements, transportation demand management and transportation systems management measures, and pricing for roads and parking. There is continued debate over whether the RTP places enough emphasis on transit compared to highways. While the most recently adopted RTP has much greater emphasis on transit expenditures than past ones, some argue it is not enough and not soon enough. The RTP, however, is updated every four years, allowing the region to recalibrate its transportation funding priorities regularly to implement its RCP and sustainability goals.

Since SANDAG does not have land-use authority, the local jurisdictions manage land use through their comprehensive plans and zoning regulations. As jurisdictions in the San Diego region update their plans, they coordinate with SANDAG so that their plans and the RCP are consistent, and they develop their own sustainable community goals and policies to comply with AB32 and SB375. Because local officials participated in SANDAG's planning decisions, they willingly coordinate their plans with the regional plan. For example, the recently adopted county plan calls for rezoning undeveloped rural areas to direct growth to existing villages, and suburban cities are updating their general plans to direct future growth to regional transit locations. The City of San Diego updated its general plan in 2008 to carry out a "City of Villages" strategy that informs and implements the regional plan, receiving APA's 2010 Daniel Burnham Award for Comprehensive Planning. Under the city's planning system, its general plan is coordinated with community plans at the neighborhood scale and with master plans at the major discretionary subdivision scale. (For a more complete description of the San Diego city plans, see Appendix B.)

The San Diego Regional Comprehensive Plan exemplifies the principles of planning for sustainable places. It demonstrates the possibilities of building a large-scale system of nested plans with a common focus on sustainability, where regional consensus has been developed through a pragmatic combination of inclusive participation and targeted funding. It illustrates the impacts of acquiring implementation power through a historic process of regionwide voter initiatives aimed at managing growth and dealing with recognized stakeholder concerns, such as congestion and environmental quality.

SAN DIEGO REGIONAL COMPREHENSIVE PLAN SCORECARD

	Low	Moderate	High
Livable Built Environment. The Sustainable Communities Strategy and the Smart Growth Concept Map guide future growth to compact areas served by transit and public facilities.			X
Harmony with Nature. The Habitat Conservation Plans (HCPs) protect complete biological communities, rather than individual endangered species.			X
Resilient Economy. The regional comprehensive plan lays out regional economic development strategies around targeted industry clusters and identifies regional infrastructure funding needs.			X
Interwoven Equity. The Regional Housing Needs Assessment sets capacity for affordable housing.			X
Healthy Community. The Sustainable Communities Strategy aims to reduce GHG emissions to meet regional goals set by the state.			X
Responsible Regionalism. Local jurisdictions participate extensively in regional-planning goal setting, and the theme of sustainability permeates both regional and local planning.			X
Authentic Participation. Regional institutions conduct extensive public outreach as part of the Sustainable Communities Strategy.			X
Accountable Implementation. A multipronged implementation program allocates transportation and environmental funding in accordance with priorities and goals in the regional comprehensive plan and the regional transportation plan.			X

KEENE, NEW HAMPSHIRE, 2010 COMPREHENSIVE MASTER PLAN

Keene is the largest city in southwestern New Hampshire. The city's population has grown slowly but steadily since 1970. This growth rate is expected to continue in subsequent years; by 2030, Keene's population will be approximately 25,220. As the hub of the region, Keene provides services, programs, and resources for a much greater population than the residents of the city alone.

Over the last decade, Keene has worked to address sustainability through climate protection measures to lower GHG emissions and to increase community resiliency to the expected impacts associated with a changing climate. In 2010, Keene updated its collection of existing master plans by adopting one plan—a comprehensive master plan (www. ci.keene.nh.us/departments/planning/keene-cmp-2010/plan).

Vision Focus Areas

Keene's plan vision is supported by six vision focus areas that frame an adaptive response to climate change and a proactive approach to sustainability.

1. A quality built environment. The built environment focus addresses the physical and structural parts of the city, including:

- providing quality housing;
- sustaining a vibrant downtown;
- maintaining neighborhoods;
- preserving and celebrating architectural history;
- balancing growth and the provision of infrastructure;
- providing a complete transportation system; and
- fostering renewable energy and the efficient use of resources.

2. A unique natural environment. The natural environment focus addresses the natural elements (green spaces, plants and animals, hillsides and waterways) within and around the city, as well as the man-made areas (green infrastructure, parks, agriculture, and gardens). Topics addressed in this section include achieving community sustainability and creating green infrastructure.

3. A vibrant economy. The economy focus addresses the issues of opportunity, prosperity, livability, and meaningful work for citizens. Topics include providing for a balanced local economy and creating employment opportunities.

4. A strong citizenship and proactive leadership. This section focuses on how community members are engaged in civic opportunities. Topics addressed include:
- transparent and responsive leadership;
- collaborative community planning; and
- engaged citizenry.

5. A creative, learning culture. This section of the plan focuses on how a creative, learning culture can foster individual and community health and well-being, education, and interpersonal relationships. The topics addressed by this section include:

- thriving arts and culture;
- educational opportunities for all; and
- diversity.

6. A healthy community. This section of the plan focuses on how a healthy and safe community can provide for community and individual health and well-being, access to health-care opportunities, and resources to lead safe, healthy lives. The topics addressed include:

- healthy living;
- public safety; and
- social services.

VISION FOCUS AREAS IN THE KEENE, NEW HAMPSHIRE, 2010 PLAN

Keene's plan vision is supported by six vision focus areas that frame an adaptive response to climate change and a proactive approach to sustainability. The six areas are:

- A quality built environment

- A unique natural environment

- A vibrant economy

- A strong citizenship and proactive leadership

- A creative learning culture

- A healthy community

In addition to these focus areas, the plan also addresses a wide range of topics such as the downtown, housing, walkability, neighborhoods, arts and culture, education, and diversity.

The Plan-Making Process

In January 2008, the Keene City Council and Planning Board began a community-based planning process to create the comprehensive master plan. A steering committee was created to work closely with the planning department staff and a consultant for each phase of the process. The first step in the process was to create a cohesive community vision devised by its citizens. A series of public workshops, called Keene Voices, was structured around the six focus areas above. Each workshop began with an overview of issues and opportunities as they related to the focus area, followed by small group discussions to identify ways that the community and city could begin to achieve its goals. The second step was to use the vision as a foundation to create the plan. The committee then drafted the details of the plan, reviewing, revising, and elaborating on the goals, objectives, and actions. Breaking the project into these two phases resulted in a community-owned, city-supported initiative, with extensive participation from both community residents and people from surrounding towns and neighboring states. The public's comments, suggestions, and stated preferences assisted the steering committee in identifying and maintaining a balanced approach and a range of actions to achieve the community's vision.

Plan Implementation

The plan includes a targeted set of strategies for the subtopics within each of the six vision focus areas. The strategies are written in an easy-to-understand narrative format.

These implementation strategies are presented in the plan, along with a host of policies and actions. The plan calls for new downtown development and the accommodation of future growth through infill development; a return to density and downtown building heights closer to what existed in the town's past; adaptive reuse of historic strictures; new efforts to promote affordable housing, green buildings, and walkability; new bike paths and lanes; and a new forestry program, among others. Many of these proposed strategies find expression in the plan's future land-use map, which identifies primary urban growth areas, as well as outlying areas to be conserved and to serve as transfer-of-development rights (TDR) sending zones.

The plan's section on implementation strategies, like the overall plan, is strongly framed by a stated commitment to community sustainability. An opening section offers a definition of what a sustainable community is, quoting Aldo Leopold. The last sentence of the plan returns to this theme: "Together, we move forward from here toward a sustainable community."

The plan recognizes that strategies will need to evolve as the community works to attain its goals, and it recommends that the plan be reviewed annually, before the creation of the annual capital improvement program and operating budget. This would allow decision makers to assess progress and to adjust implementation measures to address new and revised priorities and changing circumstances.

One weakness of the plan is that it does not include nor is it accompanied by a plan-monitoring program; rather, this is identified as a task to be undertaken in the future: "To ensure the plan's success and longevity, the city and community should establish a way to monitor progress made in implementing the goals and strategies."

Overall, the plan is a good example of a new comprehensive plan built from the ground up to address sustainability principles while still incorporating efforts already made by the community, such as climate change programs. While the city will need to go further to implement and to monitor progress, the plan should serve as a good foundation.

KEENE COMPREHENSIVE MASTER PLAN SCORECARD

	Low	Moderate	High
Livable Built Environment. The plan does a particularly good job of addressing all aspects of the city's built environment and links development patterns to open space, transportation, housing, and green building, among other topics.			X
Harmony with Nature. The plan does a reasonable job of addressing environmental planning aspects and is particularly strong in addressing climate change. Keene has developed a Local Action Climate Plan to identify ways the greater community can help lower GHG emissions. The city and community, led by its CCP Committee, have developed processes and implemented projects to ensure that they are on track to meet their GHG emissions reduction goal of 10 percent below 1995 levels by 2015.		X	
Resilient Economy. The plan has a strong and thoughtfully written economic development element based on community and business surveys and strong sustainable economic principles.			X
Interwoven Equity. The plan emphasizes civic and community involvement in decision making; it also addresses affordable and workforce housing, poverty, homelessness, and food access and security.			X
Healthy Community. The plan includes a dedicated section to this topic, emphasizing healthy food, an active community, and safety.			X
Responsible Regionalism. The plan has good recognition of regional considerations in its introduction.		X	
Authentic Participation. The plan encourages a very robust community involvement process in preparing the vision and plan.			X
Accountable Implementation. The plan leaves measuring and monitoring as a future goal.	X		

BURLINGTON, VERMONT, 2000 LEGACY PLAN

Burlington is the largest city in Vermont and is the hub of the Burlington–South Burlington metropolitan area. In 2000, Burlington created a 2030 sustainability plan, the Legacy Plan (http://burlingtonlegacyproject.org/files/2009/06/LegacyActionPlan.pdf), with input from hundreds of residents and other stakeholders. This 48-page plan serves as a road map for the community's future and is a good illustration of a succinct sustainability-based comprehensive plan. The following are the foundational principles of the plan:

- Maintaining Burlington as a regional population, government, cultural, and economic center with livable-wage jobs, full employment, social supports, and housing that matches job growth and family income
- Improving the quality of life in neighborhoods
- Increasing participation in community decision making
- Providing youth with high-quality education and social supports, as well as lifelong learning opportunities for all
- Preserving environmental health

The goals of the Legacy Plan include high-quality education for all, a healthy natural environment, strong economic growth, and a commitment to social equity. Since the plan was written, addressing the impacts of climate change has emerged as a major challenge

BURLINGTON LEGACY PLAN

Burlington's Legacy Plan is a living document that was adopted in 2000 and has led to a series of follow-up initiatives. The plan was created with intensive public participation as well as coordination among the various sectors of the community in advancing the vision of the city. The community evaluates the plan annually, and a score is given for measuring progress toward reaching each of the plan's five major goals.

to realizing the plan's vision, but this challenge is also an opportunity. For example, reducing harmful emissions can lead to job creation, cost savings, improved public health, and cleaner air and water.

The plan provides a good range of goals and actions illustrative of the broader content of sustainable comprehensive plans, which may be a model for all new comprehensive plans. In comparison with more traditional comprehensive plans, the Legacy Plan is evolving in stages—starting with an overview plan and vision, then moving to more detailed action plans such as a climate action plan (http://burlingtonclimateaction.com/climate-action-plan/towards-a-sustainable-future). This is a more effective product and process than more traditional comprehensive plans, which often have a narrower land-use focus and attempt to move from goals to details all in one document.

The Plan-Making Process

The process of building the Legacy Plan and working with the community began in 1999 and was headed by the mayor with help from a mayoral steering committee. The Legacy Plan is built on a foundation of broad stakeholder input and involved many different outreach strategies and techniques. For example, a youth delegation was formed to integrate the voices and concerns of younger community members, and Neighborhood Planning Assembly meetings were used to reach residents in each of the city's seven wards. This participatory process took 12 months to complete, leading to the plan's approval in 2000.

Measurement and Evaluation

The Legacy Project uses indicator data (http://burlingtonlegacyproject.org/about-us/indicators) to illustrate and to measure the successes and shortcomings in realizing the vision, and the group hosts an annual town meeting where projects and initiatives throughout the year are celebrated and the goals and metrics in the plan are reviewed. The information for evaluation is gathered from various city departments, the private sector, and the public sector, including the city's key institutions and steering committee members.

There are multiple cases of the Legacy Project achieving its goals and objectives. For example, Burlington has added to its stock of subsidized, affordable housing, decreased its energy use to mid-1980s levels, and launched a local food production effort with a Farm-to-School program. In 2010, the Burlington Legacy Plan was recognized with a Home Depot Foundation Sustainable Community Development Award.

While major strides have been made, more work is required in multiple areas of the five themes that require more coordination, creativity, and research before 2030. In the 2010 Burlington Town Meeting, the Legacy Project unveiled its Report Card 2010 (http://burlingtonlegacyproject.org/files/2010/03/reportcardprintable.pdf), based on the input of "sector specialists," and included initial rankings of the project's work on the five chapters of the plan. For each theme, a score from 1 to 5 was given, 5 being "accomplished," and 1 being "unaccomplished." "Governance" and "neighborhoods" were the lowest-scoring categories (2.0 and 2.5, respectively), while the other three received a score of 3.0. The overall grade for the progress of the Burlington Legacy Project is 2.5.

In addition to the report card and town meeting each year, institutional members of the steering committee and city departments make annual commitments to the plan. For example, department heads are asked to review the plan and commit to and report back on specific projects or actions to realize the 2030 goals. However, it is unclear how a fiscal evaluation is made in prioritizing initiatives or how difficult choices are made.

The Burlington Legacy Project is a fine example of a concerted and coordinated effort of a city focusing its resources and community efforts toward achievable and measurable results for a sustainable future.

BURLINGTON LEGACY PLAN SCORECARD

	Low	Moderate	High
Livable Built Environment. Not a particularly strong point of the plan.	X		
Harmony with Nature. The plan touches upon environmental aspects but not in great detail; the Climate Action Plan and other more recent initiatives take a more targeted approach.		X	
Resilient Economy. Two of the four goals of the plan focus on the economy; the city has an adopted environmentally preferred purchasing policy.			X
Interwoven Equity. The plan emphasizes the importance of young people and community involvement in decision making.		X	
Healthy Community. The focus is on improved nutrition in schools.		X	
Responsible Regionalism. Not emphasized in this plan.	X		
Authentic Participation. The plan is strong on public participation and coordination at all levels.			X
Accountable Implementation. The plan has a strong emphasis on measuring and monitoring results.			X

UNION COUNTY, PENNSYLVANIA, CULTIVATING COMMUNITY COMPREHENSIVE PLAN

Union County is a rural and small-town county located in central Pennsylvania on the Susquehanna River north of Harrisburg. Prepared through a two-year planning process with extensive public participation, Cultivating Community: A Plan for Union County's Future was adopted by the Board of County Commissioners in December 2009. It is both a countywide comprehensive plan that defines goals and strategies at the county level and a series of multimunicipal plans defining more specific actions to be taken by municipalities within three joint-planning areas to implement those goals and strategies.

A statistically valid survey conducted early in the planning process determined that residents consider energy conservation, growth management, improved roadways and transportation, low tax rates, and employment opportunities to be the most important issues facing Union County. Based on public input from the survey, meetings, and other outreach, principles were established to provide the plan's direction to achieve sustainable future growth. The sustainability principles are:

1. Focus new development in and around established communities.
   - Promote reinvestment in existing towns and villages.
   - Develop in proximity to existing infrastructure.
2. Preserve rural resources.
   - Maintain prime farmland soils and limit the impact of new development on agriculture.
   - Preserve sensitive natural features and scenic views.
3. Conserve energy.
   - Decrease fossil fuel consumption.
   - Reduce automobile use and promote transportation alternatives.
4. Conserve fiscal resources.
   - Limit the negative impacts of new development on municipal budgets.
   - Limit the negative impacts of new development on community services.

 UNION COUNTY CULTIVATING COMMUNITY PLAN

The Union County plan's sustainability principles are:

1. Focus new development in and around established communities.
2. Preserve rural resources.
3. Conserve energy.
4. Conserve fiscal resources.

The plan is divided into three sections: the Vision and Framework for the Future, Comprehensive Plan Elements, and Partnerships for Implementation. The vision section emphasizes protection of the county's rural, small-town character and agricultural and natural resources, together with sustainable economic development. It includes a growth management strategy that directs most new development to designated growth areas in Union County's boroughs and villages and away from rural resource areas (agricultural and forest lands).

The comprehensive plan elements define goals and strategies for topical elements as required by the Pennsylvania Municipalities Planning Code. "Sustainability keys" are identified for each element to set the direction for implementation. The seven elements and their sustainability keys are:

1. Natural and agricultural resources—system integrity

2. Land use—mixed use

3. Housing—diversity

4. Economic development—building local assets

5. Transportation—multimodal transportation choices

6. Cultural, historic, and recreational resources—adaptive reuse

7. Community facilities, utilities, and energy conservation—energy conservation

The implementation section includes a countywide action plan, action plans for the three multimunicipal planning areas, and a plan-monitoring program. A table on plan interrelationships identifies connections among the sustainability keys for the different elements. The plan-monitoring program identifies sample sustainability indicators tied to the keys and proposes that Union County partner with the Bucknell University Environmental Center to establish definitive indicators and responsibilities for monitoring and updating them on a yearly basis.

The Cultivating Community plan is an example of planning by a rural jurisdiction with relatively modest resources that incorporated a deliberate focus on sustainability into its comprehensive planning process. Community engagement throughout the process resulted in a vision, principles, and actions to achieve a sustainable future that directly reflect the values and priorities of Union County residents. While the plan is structured into conventional elements as required by the state code, the sustainability principles and keys serve to integrate the different elements. Cultivating Community received the 2010 Daniel Burnham Award for a Comprehensive Plan from the Pennsylvania Chapter of APA.

CULTIVATING COMMUNITY: A PLAN FOR UNION COUNTY'S FUTURE SCORECARD

	Low	Moderate	High
Livable Built Environment. The plan emphasizes multimodal transportation choices (with a focus on walkability, pedestrianism, and bicycle systems), mixed use development, housing diversity, green building, and renewable energy.			X
Harmony with Nature. The plan addresses land conservation, stewardship of natural resources, and maintaining the integrity of environmental systems.			X
Resilient Economy. Economic development based on local resources is a major theme of the plan. It proposes managing growth to maintain fiscal sustainability, promoting asset-based development, and partnering with local educational and health-are institutions in economic development initiatives.			X
Interwoven Equity. The Housing element addresses affordable housing. The Community Facilities element addresses access to health care and community services.		X	
Healthy Community. The plan promotes local agriculture and access to locally grown foods; walkable environments; accessible parks and greenways; access to health care services; and protection of historic resources.			X
Responsible Regionalism. The plan has a strong emphasis on regional approaches within Union County (multimunicipal planning, regionalization of services, etc.). It provides limited direction on coordination with surrounding jurisdictions.		X	
Authentic Participation. A broad and open participation process was used to develop the plan, including techniques geared to different population groups (e.g., Mennonites, middle-school students).			X
Accountable Implementation. The plan involved the public in setting goals and includes an implementation program with priorities for action, responsibilities, and a monitoring process including the use of indicators to measure goal achievement).			X

DRAFT OF THE PHILADELPHIA 2035 COMPREHENSIVE PLAN

Philadelphia has a long and distinguished planning history, dating back to William Penn's important 1681 plan. Penn's legacy continues with the newest proposed citywide plan, an impressive draft called Philadelphia 2035. The result of two series of public meetings in the spring and fall of 2010, as well as extensive research and analysis, the plan addresses a comprehensive set of issues and puts forth a compelling physical and policy vision for the future of the city.

▶ **PHILADELPHIA 2035
COMPREHENSIVE PLAN**

Philadelphia's population has been declining and it faces significant planning challenges. While its plan has no specific sustainability section, the concept is extensively discussed. The plan's format is innovative, organized around three major themes: Thrive, Connect, and Renew. The plan is notable in its inclusion of recommendations from two related city plans—Greenworks Philadelphia and Green City Clean Water—as well as the Delaware Valley regional plan. ◀

Philadelphia has significant planning challenges: it has been a shrinking city (by 2000, Philadelphia was down 25 percent from its peak population, but it grew modestly between 2004 and 2009 and is expected to grow from 1.55 to 1.65 million by 2035). It has a declining jobs base, significant pockets of poverty and neighborhood decline, inadequate access to healthy food in many neighborhoods, and likely significant future impacts from climate change and sea-level rise, among others.

While there is no section of the plan labeled "sustainability," the concept emerges as an important underlying current throughout the document. This begins in the prefacing letter from Mayor Michael Nutter, who discusses walkability as "just one example of our commitment to sustainability; achievements happen every day to make Philadelphia and its region healthier and more sustainable" (iii).

The heart of the content of the plan presents a series of land-use strategies and interventions, organized around three major themes: Thrive, Connect, and Renew. These themes replace the topical elements (land use, transportation, etc.) of traditional comprehensive plans and provide an innovative and compelling organization for the plan's policies, strategies, and targets.

The Thrive section argues for the importance of healthy neighborhoods in the city and calls for, among other things, redeveloping the city's former industrial sites. The plan identifies about 8,000 areas of vacant land, much of it formerly industrial, and envisions much of the city's future development happening there. Seven so-called Industrial Legacy Areas, former manufacturing areas in the city (e.g., the Navy Yard, the Central Delaware Waterfront, and Philadelphia International Airport), are identified as key growth and redevelopment areas.

The plan also advocates colocation of public services and amenities (e.g., libraries, health centers, recreational facilities) to strengthen neighborhoods. It also draws attention to the need to expand housing options for residents. The plan calls for strengthening neighborhood centers by promoting transit-oriented development (TOD). Notably, one of the main strategy areas is Access to Healthy Foods; the plan physically identifies places in the city where new grocery stores, corner stores, and farmers markets are needed, especially near transit nodes. The plan presents a comprehensive map of all points of healthy food access in the city (e.g., farmers markets, corner stores participating in the Food Trust's Healthy Corner Store Initiative).

The plan's Connect section identifies a number of key steps for improving the city's transportation system, including increasing use of and investment in public transit. The plan identifies several new transit extensions and stations and a new waterfront light-rail line. The plan recommends a Complete Streets policy to further expand mobility spaces for pedestrians and bicyclists.

Many of the plan's main green elements are contained within the Renew section. Here a number of steps are identified to strengthen and connect the city's system of parks and trails. The plan proposes a corridor network to tie together parks and trails, and it establishes the goal that every resident should be within a 10-minute walk (i.e., a quarter mile) of a neighborhood park or green area. (A map identifies areas in the city where this level of green access is not provided.) A number of creative options for providing these neighborhood green spaces are identified and mapped, including schoolyards and vacant land that might be converted to such uses as community gardens. The plan sets out targets for tree canopy coverage (an increase in overall coverage to 30 percent citywide) and more equitable distribution of trees in the city. The plan also addresses climate change and lays out fairly ambitious targets for reductions in GHG emissions: a 45 percent per capita reduction, from 1990 levels, by 2035.

The latter third of the plan addresses implementation. The plan envisions as a second phase the development of 18 district (neighborhood-scale) plans to be prepared over the next five years, in addition to revisions to the city's zoning ordinance and other codes. The plan also presents a detailed cost matrix, which estimates the capital and operating costs of all strategies developed in the plan, as well as the responsible agencies and expected time frames for implementation.

This plan has a number of exemplary qualities. It is comprehensive, nicely integrating issues of environment, economy, and community into a cohesive plan. The environmental initiatives are bold, from expanding and connecting parks and green spaces, to setting targets for GHG reduction, to tree planting, to creating more green streets in the city and pervious spaces for stormwater collection. Consistent with the focus of this report, it effectively references and integrates prior stand-alone sustainability plans, endorsing the 2009 Greenworks Philadelphia plan, which embraces the goal of making Philadelphia the greenest city in the United States by 2015. The plan also references the city's Public Works Department's Green City Clean Water plan, which contains the impressive goal of converting one-third of the area draining combined water and sewer systems into pervious surfaces of various kinds.

The plan's graphics, format, and visual qualities are striking and unusual, and they may be the key to its ultimate success with the public and other critical stakeholders expected to embrace, support, and implement the plan. By using bird's-eye visuals, the plan conveys a strong sense of the entire city, and the plan very effectively organizes the specific areas where improvements and interventions are envisioned for the future. The plan intersperses many examples of existing projects and programs, mostly within Philadelphia, throughout the text. The plan's explicit attention to and clear statement of ultimate goals is also commendable; early in the plan, it details the main economic, health, and environmental benefits to accrue from the plan actions.

The plan reflects the relatively new emphasis on public health, and it places public health goals front and center, which distinguishes it from many others. It is one of the first to integrate to a significant degree consideration of community food systems and food security. Discussion of food issues and planning strategies can be found throughout the plan; it is one of the best comprehensive plans in terms of community food content and coverage, reflecting the important role groups such as the Food Trust have played in Philadelphia.

The plan also addresses a number of elements that help to shape the unique sense of place in that city. There are proposals to protect and to build onto the city's historic assets (e.g., the Reading Viaduct Park, a concept similar to the High Line in New York City) and to strengthen the city's public realm. Impressively, the plan maps all the outdoor sculptures and murals in the city.

An explicit effort in the plan to understand and to display the relationships among different goals, objectives, and actions is also commendable. For instance, the plan includes an "Objectives Tracking Matrix" that shows the cross-cutting benefits provided by the different objectives within the plan's main Thrive, Connect, and Renew themes. A variety of specific measures and indicators for assessing the objectives are also provided.

The city has taken a number of other steps toward sustainability, including the creation of an Office of Sustainability, which is spearheading action on a range of issues from solar energy to green buildings (www.phila.gov/green). And importantly, a strong parallel regional plan—called Connections: The Regional Plan for a Sustainable Future—also exists. Prepared by the Delaware Valley Regional Planning Commission (www.dvrpc.org), this plan has an even more explicit emphasis on sustainability. The regional plan is temporally parallel with the city's plan (also aimed at 2035), and in fact the city sought to harmonize its time frame with the regional plan's. The Delaware Valley plan lays out an expansive vision for the making the region more livable, concentrating future growth around the region's existing centers, improving its multimodal transportation system, reducing GHG emissions, and shifting the region in the direction of an energy-efficient economy.

PHILADELPHIA COMPREHENSIVE PLAN SCORECARD

	Low	Moderate	High
Livable Built Environment. The plan calls for strengthening walkable qualities of the city and improving and strengthening its 170 neighborhoods; calls for major improvements in public transit; and steers most new growth into former industrial areas of the city. The plan calls for a variety of investments in new green infrastructure, including parks and neighborhood green spaces, green streets and sidewalks, and trees..			X
Harmony with Nature. The plan contains very strong and extensive environmental elements, provisions for protection of sensitive lands in the city, ambitious GHG emission targets, tree canopy targets, proposals for expanding parks (and the goal of having every resident within a 10-minute walk of a park), and a proposal for a corridor network of parks and green spaces; the plan identifies a number of opportunities for expanding neighborhood green spaces.			X
Resilient Economy. The plan boldly calls for repurposing the city's seven Industrial Legacy Areas. It contains an extensive economic development chapter, emphasizing the need to build on city assets, including growing institutional sectors (universities, hospitals) and cultural tourism.			X
Interwoven Equity. The plan strongly emphasizes neighborhood improvement, affordable and mixed-income housing, and the need to expand access to healthy food in the city.			X
Healthy Community. The plan makes a strong and clear statement of its public health goals and makes clear connections between the natural environment, access to food, walkable neighborhoods, and desired public health outcomes. There is an especially strong emphasis placed on access to healthy food and food security.			X
Responsible Regionalism. While the plan is primarily focused on the City and County of Philadelphia, it recognizes its regional context throughout. The plan states its intention to "synchronize with the vision and recommendations" of the Delaware Valley Regional Plan; and the plan chose its time frame—2035—specifically to be consistent with the time frame of the regional plan.			X
Authentic Participation. The plan reflects extensive community engagement and participation, including a series of public meetings in the spring and fall of 2010, convened at various locations around the city. Innovatively, the city organized a poster contest for all fourth, seventh, and 11th graders.			X
Accountable Implementation. The plan includes an extensive implementation component; it envisions preparation of 18 district plans and calls for revisions to the city's zoning ordinance and other codes. It also presents a detailed cost matrix, which estimates the capital and operating costs of all strategies developed in the plan, as well as the expected time frames for implementation.			X

DRAFT OF THE ALBANY, NEW YORK, 2030 COMPREHENSIVE PLAN

In July 2011, Albany, New York, released a draft of Albany 2030, the first-ever comprehensive plan for the state's capital. While the city itself has a population of just under 100,000, Albany has close ties with the nearby cities of Troy, Schenectady, and Saratoga Springs, forming a region called the Capital District, with a population of more than 850,000. The core of the draft plan is based on eight Sustainability Building Blocks, which tie together the comprehensive plan vision components into a series of eight interrelated systems, with sustainability as an overarching direction. These eight systems serve as the basis of the plan's policy framework:

1. Community form
2. Economy
3. Social
4. Transportation
5. Natural resources
6. Housing and neighborhoods
7. Utilities and infrastructure
8. Institutions

The fundamental premise of the plan is based on a systems approach, focusing on interrelationships between plan elements and topics, and the synergies that can be created by focusing on connections and linkages. The plan is expected to be adopted by the end of 2011.

Vision Components

The plan vision is based on six key components:

1. Safe, livable neighborhoods
2. Model educational system
3. Vibrant urban center
4. Multimodal transportation
5. Green city
6. Prosperous economy

Sustainability Building Blocks

The core of the plan is Chapter 3.0, Sustainability Building Blocks: The Comprehensive Plan Systems. It contains subsections that address the goals, strategies, and actions for each of the eight systems. Each of the systems is further broken down into more specific topics. For example, the Social section of the plan addresses education, community health and recreation, public safety, arts and culture, and social services.

Systems Interrelationships

The last section of Chapter 3.0, Systems Interrelationships, includes a series of tables that identify the system interconnections between goals and strategies among the different systems. These interconnections were used to identify and to prioritize actions into a series of implementation projects contained in the plan implementation section.

ALBANY SYSTEMS APPROACH

The Albany 2030 draft comprehensive plan uses a systems approach to develop the overarching direction set by its vision statement into strategies and actions for eight plan systems and priorities for implementation. Plan strategies, actions, and implementation projects are designed to optimize and to align the performance of the systems in the vision statement.

Systems thinking is used to overcome limitations of the "silo" approach that creates discrete plan elements and to help decision makers prioritize strategies and actions for implementation so as to leverage limited resources to accomplish more with less.

Plan Implementation

Albany 2030 takes a novel approach to implementation by using a systems approach to identify priorities for implementation. The prioritization process is somewhat complex and takes into account community priorities (as identified during resource allocation exercises during community outreach meetings), systems overlaps (e.g., strategies and actions that connect different plan systems), and leverage points (described as places where intervention can most effectively bring about change throughout the system, related to quality of life, increased fiscal capacity, facilitating private investment, and green community aspirations). The plan identifies a number of discrete short-, medium-, and long-term, as well as ongoing, implementation projects. Finally, the implementation section outlines a basic approach to a plan-monitoring program, including "measures of success" (indicators) for each of the plan systems, an annual review, a five-year assessment, and a 10-year update.

Linkages among Topics

A table for each of the systems topics illustrates the linkages among strategies and actions in other systems areas of the plan.

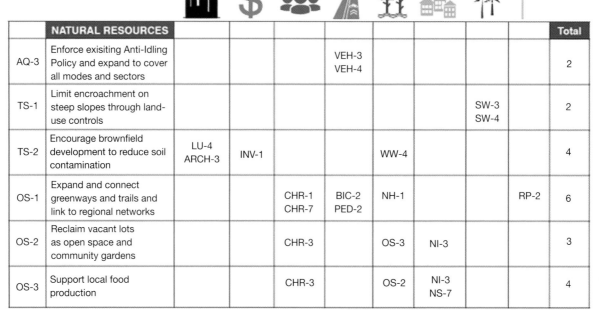

	NATURAL RESOURCES									Total
AQ-3	Enforce exisiting Anti-Idling Policy and expand to cover all modes and sectors				VEH-3 VEH-4					2
TS-1	Limit encroachment on steep slopes through land-use controls							SW-3 SW-4		2
TS-2	Encourage brownfield development to reduce soil contamination	LU-4 ARCH-3	INV-1			WW-4				4
OS-1	Expand and connect greenways and trails and link to regional networks			CHR-1 CHR-7	BIC-2 PED-2	NH-1			RP-2	6
OS-2	Reclaim vacant lots as open space and community gardens			CHR-3		OS-3	NI-3			3
OS-3	Support local food production			CHR-3		OS-2	NI-3 NS-7			4

City of Albany

ALBANY 2030 COMPREHENSIVE PLAN SCORECARD

	Low	Moderate	High
Livable Built Environment. The plan's Community Form section addresses land-use patterns, urban design, the land use/transportation connection, and built character; its transportation section addresses multimodal connections, Complete Streets, and pedestrian, bicycle, and transit needs.		X	
Harmony with Nature. The plan addresses waterways, stormwater management, brownfield sites, urban forestry, and air quality. The Utilities section addresses energy and green building, with a strong linkage to the city's Energy and Sustainability Office.			X
Resilient Economy. The plan focuses on employment opportunities and fostering partnerships to increase private-sector investments.			X
Interwoven Equity. The plan used extensive efforts during the outreach process to engage all parts of the community. There is some emphasis in the Social and Housing and Neighborhoods sections on addressing broadening needs.			X
Healthy Community. The plan addresses this criterion in the Social (community health and recreation) and Transportation sections.			X
Responsible Regionalism. The plan mentions regional economic development partnerships in the Economy section, as well as actions in the Institutions topic that address regional cooperation.			X
Authentic Participation. The planning process was completed with a robust engagement process that featured creative approaches and engaged a broadly representative section of the community.			X
Accountable Implementation. The plan strongly emphasizes specific actions to implement the plan; it has some emphasis on measuring and monitoring results.			X

CONNECTING CLEVELAND 2020 CITYWIDE PLAN

Between 1950 and 2010, Cleveland's population declined from 914,810 at its peak to under 400,000 today. The city's top job-producing sector, manufacturing, experienced a similar decline. Cleveland's previous comprehensive plan, the Civic Vision 2000 Plan (completed in 1990), presented a vision to "restructure" Cleveland as a smaller but more viable city and led to redevelopment successes in the 1990s. The Connecting Cleveland 2020 Citywide Plan (http://planning.city.cleveland.oh.us/cwp) builds on and expands prior city planning efforts, incorporating both "people-based" and "place-based" strategies. In addition to the overarching theme of connections, the plan has a major focus on environmental, economic, and social sustainability.

The plan vision calls for Cleveland in 2020 to be a national leader in biomedical and information technology; a center for advanced manufacturing; a city of safe, vibrant neighborhoods; an arts and culture mecca; and a model for healthy living and sustainable development. Guiding principles include the following:

- *Connections*: connecting people and places and opportunities
- *Assets*: building on assets in the city and each of its neighborhoods
- *Opportunity*: "reimagining" Cleveland to turn challenges into opportunities
- *Place*: creating competitive urban places with character and identity
- *Choice*: creating "communities of choice" in Cleveland for residents with many choices as well as for those with relatively few choices
- *Diversity*: embracing and celebrating diversity in people, housing, and opportunities
- *Sustainability*: building a community that is healthful and viable

The major components of Connecting Cleveland 2020 are 12 chapters for citywide application and six chapters for planning districts in different sections of the city. The topics addressed by the citywide chapters transcend the focus of traditional comprehensive plans on land-use and physical development:

- Population
- Housing
- Retail
- Economic development
- Recreation and open space
- Sustainability
- Arts and culture
- Education and community service
- Transportation and transit
- Safety
- Preservation
- Opportunity and equity

CONNECTING CLEVELAND 2020 PLAN

The vision for this city, faced with a history of decline, is to become a leader in biomedical and information technology, a center for advanced manufacturing, a city of safe, vibrant neighborhoods, an arts and culture mecca, and a model for healthy living and sustainable development. Its sustainability chapter is one of the most robust plan parts. Planning district chapters focus on clusters of neighborhoods as building blocks, each with identified development opportunities.

The sustainability chapter is one of the most robust sections of the plan, addressing a wide range of issues related to the environmental, economic, and viability of Cleveland and its region. These issues include sustainable development patterns and practices; sustainable ("full life-cycle") neighborhoods; a sustainable economy; protection of natural resources; high-performance and green building; multimodal travel; energy conservation and renewable energy; brownfield remediation; recycling and waste management; and air and water quality.

The planning district chapters are organized around clusters of neighborhoods, a structure designed to focus on each of Cleveland's 36 neighborhoods as integrated building blocks of the larger plan. Each planning district chapter provides an overview of the district and identifies assets, challenges, and development opportunities for each neighborhood located within it. The development opportunities are mapped and listed by type (arts and culture, economic development, housing, recreation, retail, or schools). Other components of the plan include a proposed 2020 land-use map; lists and maps of capital improvements (limited to transportation and transit projects); and links to funding resources and related plans (neighborhood, small area, and regional).

The Connecting 2020 Cleveland Citywide Plan is exemplary in how it incorporates sustainability principles and strategies into a nontraditional comprehensive plan structure that integrates environmental, economic, and social concerns, as well as citywide and neighborhood scales. While the plan proposes a number of actions, it lacks a separate implementation component identifying action time frames, responsible parties, and monitoring metrics and procedures. Also, the community engagement process is not documented in the plan.

CONNECTING CLEVELAND 2020 CITYWIDE PLAN SCORECARD

	Low	Moderate	High
Livable Built Environment. Creating a livable, walkable built environment is emphasized in the citywide chapters and in the strategies for individual neighborhoods outlined in the six Planning District chapters. Plan policies and strategies address housing diversity and choice; mixed use development and pedestrian-friendly design; multimodal transportation; healthy living at the neighborhood level; etc.			X
Harmony with Nature. The Sustainability and Recreation and Open Space chapters of the plan extensively address environmental issues to support the vision of Cleveland as a sustainable "Green City on a Blue Lake." Included are policies and strategies to preserve and enhance Cleveland's green infrastructure (natural areas, the urban forest, etc.); promote travel via transit, biking, and walking rather than automobile; encourage high-performance green buildings; improve air and water quality; reduce energy use and waste; etc.			X
Resilient Economy. The plan includes an Economic Development chapter that summarizes economic trends and challenges, identifies the city's key economic assets, and proposes economic development policies and strategies to build on those assets.			X
Interwoven Equity. The plan includes an Opportunity and Equity chapter focused on increasing opportunities for residents whose choices are limited by issues such as poverty, education, discrimination, and health conditions. This chapter identifies goals and policies from other plan chapters designed to provide greater opportunity and equity for all Clevelanders, "particularly those who remain near the socioeconomic bottom of the community."			X
Healthy Community. The plan identifies lifestyle-related illnesses, such as obesity and environmental degradation, that affect human health as key issues. Plan policies and strategies promote access to fresh foods; walking and other physical activity; and local food production through community gardens and urban agriculture.			X
Responsible Regionalism. The plan focuses on the City of Cleveland and does not include a specific component addressing its relationship to the Northeast Ohio region. It does, however, incorporate a regional perspective in plan directions, such as a coordinated initiative for regional economic prosperity; connections to a regional parks and open space system; and a regional approach to sustainability.		X	
Authentic Participation. The introduction to the plan notes that it "was prepared through a process that engaged thousands of Clevelanders in community groups meetings and focus groups." No further information is provided on the process used to engage citizens and stakeholders in plan development.		X	
Accountable Implementation. The plan summary identifies the importance of implementation and identifies the components of an effective implementation strategy (marketing, neighborhood connections, zoning, capital improvements, etc.). The plan does not, however, include a separate implementation chapter identifying specific actions, time frames, responsibilities, and performance measures.		X	

San Diego Regional Planning Program

William R. Anderson, FAICP, and Robert A. Leiter, FAICP

The San Diego region, coterminous with San Diego County, integrates four tiers of comprehensive plans: (1) the regional plan; (2) city plans, including the plan for unincorporated areas of the county; (3) community plans; and (4) master plans. The region is a 3.3 million–person metropolitan area within a more than 5.1-million-person binational region that includes the Tijuana-Rosarito-Ensenada metro area in Mexico. Almost 40 percent of the 4,200-square-mile region (roughly the size of Connecticut) is designated as parks and open space, including protected habitat. The City of San Diego, at 1.3 million people, is the largest of the 19 jurisdictions in the region in population, the second-largest California city, and the eighth largest in the United States. Its 343 square miles include more than 60,650 acres in open space and protected habitat. The region is projected to grow by more than 800,000 people over the next 25 years, of which more than half are expected to live within the city.

TIER 1: THE REGIONAL COMPREHENSIVE PLAN

Regional comprehensive planning began as a growth management effort and has evolved to deal with conservation and climate change issues. Voter approval of two 1988 initiatives were critical:

- The San Diego Association of Governments (SANDAG), the regional transportation planning agency, obtained authority for a half-cent sales tax for transportation (known as TransNet) that provided $3.3 billion in funding over a 20-year period for regional highway and public transit projects, along with local transportation projects and activities.

- SANDAG was designated as a "regional growth management" organization, with responsibilities to monitor and report on activities in the region that address the impacts of growth on public facilities and the environment.

At the same time, an environmental conflict was triggered by concern for 340,000 acres of coastal sage scrub occupied by the coastal California gnatcatcher, a small songbird whose range extends across Southern California. Environmentalists sought to have the gnatcatcher designated as endangered, in opposition to the development community. In response, the California legislature passed the Natural Community Conservation Planning Act (NCCP Act) in 1991 (California Fish and Game Code Section 2800–35).

This act provided for a regional planning process focused on protection of biological "communities," rather than single species, in order to conserve species before they became endangered. It established requirements for preparation of Natural Community Conservation Plans, similar to the Habitat Conservation Plans (HCPs) allowed under the federal Endangered Species Act. These plans protect sensitive plant and animal species in a designated geographic area, while allowing development of less sensitive areas. Local jurisdictions in the region's two conservation plan areas agreed to designate sensitive habitat areas for permanent preservation in order to protect 85 animal and plant species, resulting in more than 472,000 acres of preserved habitats.

In the late 1990s, SANDAG noted that current local general plans in the region would be unable to accommodate forecasted growth and were inconsistent with the Regional Growth Management Strategy. An intensive, three-year long debate on regional governance ensued. In 2002, the legislature passed Senate Bill 1703, which moderately strengthened SANDAG's authority by transferring planning and project development responsibilities from the region's two transit agencies to it and altering its governance structure. In 2003, Assembly Bill 361 was enacted, giving SANDAG the authority and the responsibility to prepare and adopt a "Regional Comprehensive Plan" (RCP) by 2004 that would incorporate public input, use the agency's authority over regional transportation funds to further the goals of the plan, and monitor progress through "realistic measurable standards and criteria" to be included in the plan.

The current RCP builds on the regional transportation plan while addressing environmental planning issues in the broader context of an overall comprehensive plan. The RCP effort was spearheaded by SANDAG's Regional Planning Committee, made up of local elected officials representing six subregions in San Diego County and advisory members representing federal, state, and regional public agencies. In addition, SANDAG was assisted in its work by a stakeholder working group, as well as a technical working group made up of local government planning directors. The chairs of both groups sat as advisory members of the Regional Planning Committee. The two-year planning process also included extensive public outreach. This committee structure endures today.

The RCP is organized like a local general plan, with a long-range vision and elements addressing transportation, land use and urban form, housing, economic development, healthy environment (including air quality, water quality, habitat conservation, and shoreline preservation), regional public facilities (including energy, water supply, and waste management), and interregional and binational issues. The plan includes a vision and element for land use because, even though SANDAG does not have regulatory authority over land use, it can encourage compatible land uses through incentives to and collaboration with local governments. The RCP also includes a five-year action plan of strategic implementation initiatives, as well as an annual performance-monitoring program. It is implemented through key strategic initiatives, including the TransNet Environmental Mitigation Program and the Smart Growth Concept Map.

- The TransNet Environmental Mitigation Program extends the existing half-cent sales tax for transportation to acquire habitat mitigation land for new transportation projects. This program mitigates the environmental impacts of transportation projects through acquisition, management, and monitoring of the open space areas in the adopted HCPs. Its budget totals $850 million, out of an overall transportation expenditure plan of $14.4 billion.

- The Smart Growth Concept Map focuses future growth to existing and planned urban areas supported by transportation investment, including transit. It identifies some 200 smart-growth opportunity areas and delineates open-space preserve areas from the region's adopted HCPs. It is used to prioritize transportation investments and to allocate regional funding for local infrastructure improvements through the TransNet Smart Growth Incentive Program and other related grant programs.

Two recent state legislative acts have a major influence on regional planning. The 2006 California Global Warming Solutions Act (AB32) sets GHG reduction targets for the entire state of California, with the goal of reaching 1990 levels by 2020. California Senate Bill 375 changes the planning process used by metropolitan planning organizations (MPOs) like SANDAG to update their Regional Transportation Plan (RTP) and the Regional Housing Needs Assessment (RHNA). Under state law, the RHNA designates housing capacity targets for regions, including capacity for potential affordable housing, which are then allocated to local jurisdictions. SB375 requires creation of a Sustainable Communities Strategy, a new element of the RTP, as one element of a larger strategy to achieve established GHG-reduction targets.

The San Diego region is the first in California required to update its RTP to conform to the requirements of SB375. SANDAG initiated this planning process in 2009, the first step in which was the development of an updated long-range regional growth forecast to 2050, with extensive input and participation by local governments and regional stakeholders. Using this updated forecast, SANDAG then tested a variety of different transportation and land-use scenarios that included GHG-reduction measures based on the following categories:

- Land-use measures (strategies leading to more compact development, particularly near existing and future public transit)

- Transportation system improvements (focusing on public transit, bicycle facilities, and pedestrian facilities)
- Transportation demand management (TDM) and transportation system management (TSM) measures
- Pricing measures (including road pricing and parking pricing)

SANDAG's draft RTP attains the GHG-reduction targets established for the San Diego region. Its implementation will require close coordination between SANDAG and its local government partners because many of the reduction measures rely on a continuation of trends toward more compact development now reflected in many of the local general plans. While the RCP is coordinated with each jurisdiction's comprehensive or general plan and, in fact, was developed with significant input from each local jurisdiction, the RCP and SANDAG do not have land-use authority under state law. That resides with the local jurisdictions. SANDAG's primary tool for implementing the RCP is the purse, particularly for regional transportation infrastructure and habitat acquisition, as well as the application of state environmental laws, such as AB32 and SB375.

TIER 2: GENERAL PLANS OF LOCAL JURISDICTIONS

Land-use authority rests with local jurisdictions, which must prepare long-range comprehensive plans (general plans) that guide development and planning for a 20- to 25-year horizon. General plans must address land use, circulation, housing, conservation, noise, and safety elements. Jurisdictions may add other elements, such as recreation, economic prosperity, arts and culture, public facilities, and so on. Some choose to add a sustainability element, while others address sustainability in their conservation elements or throughout the general plan. General plans are the policy basis for zoning. By state law, a jurisdiction's capital improvement program (CIP) must be consistent with its general plan. While general plans are prepared every couple of decades, jurisdictions must update their housing elements every five to eight years, in accordance with state housing law.

Many jurisdictions in the San Diego region are updating their general plans to address sustainability policies and to be consistent with the RCP. Their willingness to coordinate with the RCP is a natural extension of SANDAG's consensus decision-making structure, comprising elected officials from the local jurisdictions. The region's planning directors and transportation department directors provide input through SANDAG's technical advisory committees. Regional nongovernmental organizations and nonmember agencies also participate in the committee structure. The regional HCPs, the RTP, the Smart Growth Concept Map, and the RCP are all prepared with extensive input and review by local jurisdictions.

The County of San Diego's general plan update for the unincorporated county downzones currently undeveloped rural areas to direct growth to existing rural village areas. Escondido, San Marcos, National City, and Encinitas—suburban cities—are updating their general plans to direct future growth near their regional transit stations. Chula Vista, the region's second-largest city, updated its general plan a few years ago to incorporate a Smart Growth strategy for its eastern new town, called Otay Ranch, and to accommodate infill mixed use and redevelopment in its older western neighborhoods to support the regional trolley and planned bus rapid transit system.

In accordance with the regional plan, the City of San Diego updated its general plan in 2008 (www.sandiego.gov/planning/genplan). Based on the "City of Villages" strategy, the plan received the 2010 Daniel Burnham Award for Comprehensive Planning from APA. The plan envisions a city with more housing and travel choices; pedestrian linkages to schools, parks, and centers; preserved natural landforms and open spaces; economic development that benefits the environment; buildings that are built "green" and operated efficiently; and heightened levels of water and resource conservation. The City of Villages strategy focuses growth into mixed use villages of different scales that are linked to the regional transit system, while preserving open spaces and other areas where no change is desired. Each village will be unique to its community, yet all villages will be pedestrian friendly and characterized by inviting, accessible, and attractive streets and public spaces.

Villages are designed to allow for many local trips to be made on foot or bicycle, with easy transit access to job centers and other, more distant destinations. Reducing dependence on automobiles reduces vehicle-miles traveled, which, in turn, lowers GHG emissions. Public health also benefits from walkable communities since regular exercise (walking) is integrated into everyday life. San Diego has many examples of walkable villages, such as the Hillcrest and Little Italy neighborhoods and the Village of La Jolla. Newer village developments include Liberty Station at the former Naval Training Center, the Promenade development surrounding the Rio Vista Trolley Station in Mission Valley, and the Village Center at the Euclid Avenue and Market Street Trolley Station. In these villages, people do not have to think about driving less—it is a natural by-product of the way their neighborhoods are designed.

Promotion of a balanced, multimodal transportation system that serves pedestrians, bicyclists, transit riders, and motorists is a fundamental tenet of the San Diego general plan's approach to sustainability. Transit cannot serve all areas due to limited funds, but strides can be made toward reducing auto dependence through citywide investments to improve walking and cycling connections. While politically difficult to implement, tailored parking management and pricing in certain locations are proven tools to reduce vehicle-miles traveled and to encourage more walking and transit use.

TIER 3: COMMUNITY PLANS

The City of San Diego's general plan presents citywide policies, while community plans, which are technically components of the general plan, focus these policies specifically to the context and vision of individual communities, including the land-use policies for specific parcels and the public facilities to be financed and incorporated into the CIP. Community plans are prepared with extensive community participation and are designed to guide a community's evolution over a 15- to 20-year period. San Diego is divided into more than 40 community plan areas, most of which have an associated community planning group that advises the planning commission, mayor, and city council on development and plan amendment proposals. Community planning groups are official organizations sanctioned by the city council and operate under their own bylaws in accordance with council policy. They are elected at an annual caucus in the community.

Community plans express the community's vision, goals, and policies and are organized like the general plan, though they may add elements related to particular local planning issues. Each community plan is adopted with a zoning package that implements the policies; a public facilities financing plan that identifies the funding strategy for public facilities and infrastructure specified in the plan and is also the basis for development impact fees or benefit assessments; and a program environmental impact report (PEIR). In general, proposed developments consistent with the community plan can be approved either ministerially or through a range of lower-level discretionary processes that vary in cost and complexity. CIP projects must be consistent with the community plan. Private and public projects that propose major changes to the community plan require a higher-level discretionary review process, sometimes a plan amendment, and additional environmental impact analysis. Higher-level review processes require planning commission and possibly city council action.

The general plan's sustainability policies are applied directly to the community through the community plan. These may include specific identification of Complete Streets and green streets; habitat preservation areas and interface policies; density bonuses and performance zoning criteria; reduced parking ratios to support affordable housing; potential historic districts and conservation areas; bicycle and pedestrian networks; transit-oriented development and mixed use areas; and village locations and characteristics. Once completed, community plans position a community for regional transportation funding in accordance with the RTP and RCP criteria and other Smart Growth and sustainability grants.

TIER 4: MASTER PLANS

Master plans or specific plans, while not as comprehensive as the larger-scale regional, city, and community plans, incorporate sustainability policies into physical projects that people can touch and experience. While not required for development that can build by right, they are often used with a planned unit development or site development permit for larger-scale, multiuse developments and, therefore, play an important role in planning for sustainability.

Two recent examples of sustainable master plans in the City of San Diego are Civita in the Mission Valley Community Plan area and Village at Market Creek in the Southeastern Community Plan area. Both required amendments to their respective community plans to maintain consistency with the city's general plan. Both are large-scale infill developments. Civita is the conversion of an old quarry site, and Village at Market Creek is a former brownfield site. Both master plans were designated by the state's Strategic Growth Council as "Gold Standard Catalyst Communities," conveying certain grant-scoring priorities and direct grant funding.

THE VERTICALLY INTEGRATED PLANNING SYSTEM

The San Diego system is one of several examples of vertically integrating comprehensive plans to achieve sustainable outcomes. The RCP and the RTP are designed to reduce GHG emissions by reducing vehicle-miles traveled through the design and funding of a multimodal transportation system and coordination of the regional habitat preservation systems. The general plans of the cities and county provide the supportive land-use policies for sustainable development, including transit orientation, walkability, and sustainable design. The community plans in the larger jurisdictions provide more specific policies for sustaining places, consistent with their respective general plans. Master plans bring tangible form and development to sustainable neighborhoods, structures, and public places, consistent with community plans and general plans.

This regional system is enabled by a combination of financing incentives, regulations, and consensus-building decision-making processes. The system itself is sustained by state and local laws, environmental analysis, and public participation and scrutiny. The rate at which this system is implemented depends on continued financial support and political will. The result of this comprehensive planning at nested scales will eventually combine to create a sustainable region with sustainable cities, communities, and projects. While specific to California state laws and programs, the San Diego Regional Plan offers a possible model of integrated planning, participation, and creative funding to other regions interested in large-scale sustainability.

References

American Planning Association (APA). 2000. *Policy Guide on Planning for Sustainability*. Chicago: APA.

———. 2002. *Policy Guide on Smart Growth*. Chicago: APA.

———. 2011. *Policy Guide on Climate Change*. Chicago: APA.

Beatley, Timothy. 2010. *Biophilic Cities: Integrating Nature into Urban Design and Planning*. Washington, D.C.: Island Press.

Berke, Philip R., and Maria Manta Conroy. 2000. "Are We Planning for Sustainable Development? An Evaluation of 30 Comprehensive Plans." *Journal of the American Planning Association* 66 (winter): 21–33.

Berke, Philip R., and David R. Godschalk. 2009. "Searching for the Good Plan: A Meta-Analysis of Plan Quality Studies." *Journal of Planning Literature* 23(3): 227–40.

Brown, Lester. 2009. *Plan B 4.0: Mobilizing to Save Civilization*. Washington, D.C.: Earth Policy Institute. Available at www.earth-policy.org/index.php?/books/pb4/pb4_table_of_contents.

Dunn, Alexandra Dapolito. 2010. "Siting Green Infrastructure: Legal and Policy Solutions to Alleviate Urban Poverty and Promote Healthy Communities." Paper no. 559. New York: Pace University Law Faculty Publications.

Ewing, Reid, Keith Bartholomew, Steve Winkelman, Jerry Walters, Don Chen, Barbara McCann, and David Goldberg. 2007. *Growing Cooler: The Evidence on Urban Development and Climate Change*. Washington, D.C.: Urban Land Institute.

Faga, Barbara. 2006. *Designing Public Consensus: The Civic Theater of Community Participation for Architects, Landscape Architects, Planners, and Urban Designers*. New York: John Wiley and Sons.

Feiden, Wayne. 2011. *Assessing Sustainability: A Guide for Local Governments*. Planning Advisory Service Report no. 565. Chicago: American Planning Association.

Fridley, David. 2010. "Nine Challenges of Alternative Energy." In *The Post Carbon Reader: Managing the 21st Century's Sustainability Crises*, ed. Richard Heinberg and Daniel Lerch. Healdsburg, Calif.: Watershed Media.

Godschalk, David R. 2004. "Land Use Planning Challenges: Coping with Conflicts in Visions of Sustainable Development and Livable Communities." *Journal of the American Planning Association* 70 (winter): 5–13.

Godschalk, David R., Adam Rose, Elliott Mittler, Keith Porter, and Carol Taylor West. 2009. "Estimating the Value of Foresight: Aggregate Analysis of Natural Hazard Mitigation Benefits and Costs." *Environmental Planning and Management* 52(6): 739–56.

Hancock, Trevor. 2008. "Ecological Footprint." In *Encyclopedia of Public Health*, ed. Wilhelm Kirch. New York: Springer.

Heinberg, Richard, and David Fridley. 2010. "The End of Cheap Coal." *Nature*, November 18: 367–69.

Herman, Benjamin A. 2010. "Embracing Sustainability in Community Plans." *Planning*, April.

Hollander, Justin B. 2011. *Sunburnt Cities: The Great Recession, Depopulation, and Urban Planning in the American Sunbelt*. New York: Routledge.

International Energy Agency (IEA). 2010. *World Energy Outlook 2010 Executive Summary*. Available at www.worldenergyoutlook.org/docs/weo2010/WEO2010_ES_English.pdf.

Jacobson, T., and A. Hinds. 2008. "Local Government Planning for Sustainable Development: An Evolution in California." Paper presented at the ACSP/AESOP Conference, Chicago, July.

Kenway, S. J., G. M. Turner, S. Cook, and T. Baynes. 2008. *Water-Energy Futures for Melbourne: The Effect of Water Strategies, Water Use and Urban Form*. Water for a Healthy Country flagship report. October. Clayton South, Victoria, Australia: CSIRO.

Lerch, Daniel. 2007. *Post Carbon Cities: Planning for Energy and Climate Uncertainty*. Santa Rosa, Calif.: Post Carbon Institute.

Louv, Richard. 2005. *Last Child in the Woods: Saving Our Children from Nature-Deficit Disorder*. Chapel Hill, N.C.: Algonquin.

Meck, Stuart, general ed. 2002. *Growing Smart Legislative Guidebook: Model Statutes for Planning and the Management of Change*. Chicago: American Planning Association.

Norton, Richard K. 2008. "Using Content Analysis to Evaluate Local Master Plans and Zoning Codes." *Land Use Policy* 25: 432–54.

Pilkey, O., and R. Young. 2009. *The Rising Sea*. Washington, D.C.: Island Press.

Quay, Ray. 2010. "Anticipatory Governance: A Tool for Climate Change Adaptation," *Journal of the American Planning Association* 77 (autumn): 496–511.

San Diego County Water Authority (SDCWA). n.d. "San Diego County's Water Sources." Available at www.sdcwa.org/san-diego-county-water-sources.

Schilling, Joseph. 2010. "The Promise of Sustainability Planning for Regenerating Distressed, Older Industrial Cities." Paper presented at the ACSP conference, Minneapolis, October.

Schilling, Joseph, and Jonathan Logan. 2008. "Greening the Rust Belt: A Green Infrastructure Model for Right Sizing America's' Shrinking Cities." *Journal of the American Planning Association* 74(4): 451–66.

Sheehan, Bill, and Helen Spiegelman. 2010. "Climate Change, Peak Oil, and the End of Waste." In *The Post Carbon Reader: Managing the 21st Century's Sustainability Crises*, ed. Richard Heinberg and Daniel Lerch. Healdsburg, Calif.: Watershed Media.

Smart Growth Network. 2002. *Getting to Smart Growth: 100 Policies for Implementation*. Available at www.smartgrowth.org/pdf/gettosg.pdf.

U.S. Environmental Protection Agency (EPA). 2001. *Our Built and Natural Environments: A Technical Review of the Interactions between Land Use, Transportation, and Environmental Quality*. Available at www.epa.gov/smartgrowth/built.htm.

Wackernagel, Mathis, and William Rees. 1998. *Our Ecological Footprint: Reducing Human Impact on the Earth*. Gabriola Island, B.C.: New Society.

APA American Planning Association

Making Great Communities Happen

The American Planning Association provides leadership in the development of vital communities by advocating excellence in community planning, promoting education and citizen empowerment, and providing the tools and support necessary to effect positive change.

525. E-Government. Jennifer Evans-Cowley and Maria Manta Conroy. May 2004. 41pp.

526. Codifying New Urbanism. Congress for the New Urbanism. May 2004. 97pp.

527. Street Graphics and the Law. Daniel Mandelker with Andrew Bertucci and William Ewald. August 2004. 133pp.

528. Too Big, Boring, or Ugly: Planning and Design Tools to Combat Monotony, the Too-big House, and Teardowns. Lane Kendig. December 2004. 103pp.

529/530. Planning for Wildfires. James Schwab and Stuart Meck. February 2005. 126pp.

531. Planning for the Unexpected: Land-Use Development and Risk. Laurie Johnson, Laura Dwelley Samant, and Suzanne Frew. February 2005. 59pp.

532. Parking Cash Out. Donald C. Shoup. March 2005. 119pp.

533/534. Landslide Hazards and Planning. James C. Schwab, Paula L. Gori, and Sanjay Jeer, Project Editors. September 2005. 209pp.

535. The Four Supreme Court Land-Use Decisions of 2005: Separating Fact from Fiction. August 2005. 193pp.

536. Placemaking on a Budget: Improving Small Towns, Neighborhoods, and Downtowns Without Spending a Lot of Money. Al Zelinka and Susan Jackson Harden. December 2005. 133pp.

537. Meeting the Big Box Challenge: Planning, Design, and Regulatory Strategies. Jennifer Evans-Cowley. March 2006. 69pp.

538. Project Rating/Recognition Programs for Supporting Smart Growth Forms of Development. Douglas R. Porter and Matthew R. Cuddy. May 2006. 51pp.

539/540. Integrating Planning and Public Health: Tools and Strategies To Create Healthy Places. Marya Morris, General Editor. August 2006. 144pp.

541. An Economic Development Toolbox: Strategies and Methods. Terry Moore, Stuart Meck, and James Ebenhoh. October 2006. 80pp.

542. Planning Issues for On-site and Decentralized Wastewater Treatment. Wayne M. Feiden and Eric S. Winkler. November 2006. 61pp.

543/544. Planning Active Communities. Marya Morris, General Editor. December 2006. 116pp.

545. Planned Unit Developments. Daniel R. Mandelker. March 2007. 140pp.

546/547. The Land Use/Transportation Connection. Terry Moore and Paul Thorsnes, with Bruce Appleyard. June 2007. 440pp.

548. Zoning as a Barrier to Multifamily Housing Development. Garrett Knaap, Stuart Meck, Terry Moore, and Robert Parker. July 2007. 80pp.

549/550. Fair and Healthy Land Use: Environmental Justice and Planning. Craig Anthony Arnold. October 2007. 168pp.

551. From Recreation to Re-creation: New Directions in Parks and Open Space System Planning. Megan Lewis, General Editor. January 2008. 132pp.

552. Great Places in America: Great Streets and Neighborhoods, 2007 Designees. April 2008. 84pp.

553. Planners and the Census: Census 2010, ACS, Factfinder, and Understanding Growth. Christopher Williamson. July 2008. 132pp.

554. A Planners Guide to Community and Regional Food Planning: Transforming Food Environments, Facilitating Healthy Eating. Samina Raja, Branden Born, and Jessica Kozlowski Russell. August 2008. 112pp.

555. Planning the Urban Forest: Ecology, Economy, and Community Development. James C. Schwab, General Editor. January 2009. 160pp.

556. Smart Codes: Model Land-Development Regulations. Marya Morris, General Editor. April 2009. 260pp.

557. Transportation Infrastructure: The Challenges of Rebuilding America. Marlon G. Boarnet, Editor. July 2009. 128pp.

558. Planning for a New Energy and Climate Future. Scott Shuford, Suzanne Rynne, and Jan Mueller. February 2010. 160pp.

559. Complete Streets: Best Policy and Implementation Practices. Barbara McCann and Suzanne Rynne, Editors. March 2010. 144pp.

560. Hazard Mitigation: Integrating Best Practices into Planning. James C. Schwab, Editor. May 2010. 152 pp.

561. Fiscal Impact Analysis: Methodologies for Planners. L. Carson Bise II. September 2010. 68pp.

562. Planners and Planes: Airports and Land-Use Compatibility. Susan M. Schalk, with Stephanie A. D. Ward. November 2010. 72pp.

563. Urban Agriculture: Growing Healthy, Sustainable Places. Kimberley Hodgson, Marcia Caton Campbell, and Martin Bailkey. January 2011. 148pp.

564. E-Government (revised edition). Jennifer Evans-Cowley and Joseph Kitchen. April 2011. 108pp.

565. Assessing Sustainability: A Guide for Local Governments. Wayne M. Feiden, with Elisabeth Hamin. July 2011. 108pp.

566. Planning for Wind Energy. Suzanne Rynne, Larry Flowers, Eric Lantz, and Erica Heller, Editors. November 2011. 140pp.

567. Sustaining Places: The Role of the Comprehensive Plan. David R. Godschalk and William R. Anderson. January 2012. 104pp.